Here is a little mystery.

How did a trunk said to have come back from West Africa with the famous Niger explorer Mungo Park in 1797 end up with a Maori family in Petone, New Zealand? Ripeka Love would write in 1940 that this trunk was "a treasured gift from my Mother's people to her grandchildren".

And here is how it came to be so, traced through the life and loves and art of Surveyor and Engineer, Robert Park, who arrived in New Zealand in late 1839, and of his children and sometimes grandchildren.

Published in 2009 by

Te Waihora Press
102 Wildberry Street
Christchurch 8023
New Zealand

ISBN 978-0-908714-10-0

Cover design and layout: Book Design Ltd www.bookdesign.co.nz
Printed in Taiwan by Sunny Young Printing Inc.

MUNGO PARK'S TRUNK

By Nola Easdale

DEDICATION

To Athalie Watt (née Park), and to Bobs Murchison.
Now with the ancestors they searched for.

CONTENTS

FOREWORD

This tale had its beginning in a book I wrote on 19th century surveyors in New Zealand based on their art, their letters and diaries, field book notes and sketches.

Kairuri, The Measurer of Land was published in 1988 for the centenary of the founding of the New Zealand Institute of Surveyors. (Kairuri is a transliteration of the word 'ruler' to the Maori 'ruri,' while 'kai' denotes the doing. 'Ruler' of land would have been provocative!)

Robert Park was one of these surveyor/artists. Following publication of *Kairuri*, a feature writer for the *Ashburton Guardian*, Ray McCausland, wrote seeking permission to use material from *Kairuri* for an article on Park. Park had laid out Ashburton and in the last years of his life lived nearby at Winchmore. I answered 'Yes' and Ray quoted in his article a reference from my letter to Park being 'my favourite surveyor'. I had added that I hoped someday someone would do a book on Robert Park, but that it wouldn't be me. (I was busy at that time preparing for publication *Missionary and Maori*, a history of early Kerikeri in the Bay of Islands).

In 2000 we moved to Christchurch from Auckland. Casting around for a project, Robert Park came to mind. I pursued some research in a leisurely fashion, and learned then of Park's association with a Maori woman in Wellington after his first wife's death. This was intriguing information. The two children of this liason were forebears of branches of the well-known and celebrated Love and Bennett families. However, the need to research further afield and spend more time in Wellington and elsewhere did not seem possible then, and I set Mr Park aside.

A few years later I had a call from the man who had built on our section next door to our old home in Howick. He was looking for a copy of *Kairuri* (out of print) and had realised that the person who had sold him the section was the author.

This man, Tim Park, was one of the Maori descendants of Robert Park. He sent me much information which revived my interest. In fact, it became very exciting, especially after conversations with Tim's oldest sister Athalie. By this time, too, I had met Paul Deans in Christchurch, a sculptor, and descendant (as one of the renowned Deans family of Christchurch) of Robert Park through a daughter of his third family. There were one or two other curious prompts. Fate seemed to have a hand! 'Maybe after all I should write about your great-grandfather, Tim. What do you think?' 'Certainly you should' said Tim. And so I have – with the support and encouragement of many descendants of Robert's three families – his first with Mary Ann Morgan, (now Australians), his second with Terenui of Te Atiawa, and his third with Marion Hart.

One of the most fascinating aspects of my new research was reading in family papers that Robert Park was a nephew of the 18th century explorer Mungo Park. And also learning that the object on which the tale is focused is currently in the care of Te Papa Museum in Wellington – Mungo Park's Trunk.

CHAPTER 1

ST MUNGO

The story begins in Scotland. The tale of St Mungo (from whom the name 'Mungo' derives) is as wrapped around with myth as that of Mungo Park's trunk.

St Mungo 520–612 AD is the patron saint of Glasgow, Scotland. He is said to have been the illegitimate son of Thenaw, the Christian daughter of King Lot of Lothin. About to be executed for her pregnancy, she was instead cast adrift in a coracle which was washed ashore at Culross on the Fife coast. Here Mungo was born. He was fostered by St Serf at his monastery nearby. Named Kentigern, the child was given the pet name of 'Mungo' or 'dear one'. The jealousy of the other monks at Culross at length caused the young monk Mungo to flee west. At Strathclyde he founded a monastery in the Christian Kingdom of Rydderch (Roderick) Hael at 'Clasqu' (dear family) the site of modern Glasgow, and was consecrated a Bishop. For 13 years he laboured here, until an anti-Christian movement forced him into exile in ancient Cumbria, which then straddled the Borders of Scotland and England. Here he founded many more churches which are dedicated to St Kentigern.

King Rydderch was to recall Bishop Mungo to Glasgow after many years of exile and once more Christianity flourished there. St Mungo died here in 612 and his remains lie in his tomb beneath Glasgow Cathedral near the site of the original 6th century wooden church.

Some of the legends surrounding St Mungo's life are displayed on the Glasgow City Coat of Arms and a well-known rhyming conundrum speaks of his miracles:

There's the tree that never grew
There's the bird that never flew
There's the fish that never swam
There's the bell that never rang.

The 'fish' is the salmon holding a ring. A legend goes that the King of Strathclyde was enraged on discovering that a knight was wearing the ring he had given his queen. The ring was thrown in the Clyde, unbeknownst to his wife. She was told to produce the ring within three days or she would die. An appeal was made to the saintly Bishop Mungo, and a monk was dispatched to bring back a salmon. Lo!, the ring was discovered and the lady lived.

The motto on the coat-of-arms is a secular shortening from a sermon of Bishop Mungo, when he prayed 'Lord, let Glasgow flourish by the preaching of the word', and is inscribed on the bell.

Glasgow was to flourish and the Park family who had lived about here for some generations had their fortunes mirrored in this success.

The City of Glasgow Coat of Arms. 'The fish that never swam.'
The salmon holds the Queen's ring as St Mungo had foretold.

CHAPTER 2

GLASGOW, ENGLAND AND AWA' TO NEW ZEALAND

O ne account of Park family history, said to have originated with Robert Park the surveyor, tells of the Park family coming from the 'debatable' land in Liddesdale on the Scottish Borders.

Whether this was so or not, by the 18th century this Park family had long been 'portioners' or farmers near Carmunnock not far south of Glasgow and one, Matthew, inherited a farm Muirside. His son John in his turn had this farm, and it was a son of his, Patrick, Robert's grandfather, who settled in Glasgow as a mason and builder. From Patrick Park the descent is certain.

Patrick Park, the mason and wright, married Agnes Davidson in 1766. From this union came two sons, Matthew in 1769, and Alexander in 1771. After Agnes died, Patrick married Elizabeth Hunter, giving the boys a much younger half-sister, Janet, in 1789.

Matthew and Alexander both followed their father Patrick in becoming masons and guild brethren. Guild brethren were master craftsmen and like all members of the many guilds, had had to serve apprenticeships of seven years. These guild members, along with merchants, were of the 'Burgess Class', and thus could be represented on the burgh's ruling body. Robert's father Matthew was admitted to the Guild in 1798 and Alexander in 1806.

Matthew Park about the time of his marriage to Catherine Lang in 1806. A companion painting of his wife was said to be with family in Australia. Its present whereabouts are unknown.

Courtesy Edward Duval.

Catherine Lang Park, widow of Matthew, in her mature years.

Courtesy Peter Love.

On 1 June, also in 1806, Matthew married Katharine or Catherine Lang (variously spelt though Catherine seems favoured later). She was a daughter of Robert Lang, a wood merchant, and Katharine. Matthew and Catherine were wed in her home town of Hamilton, south-east of Glasgow. They were to have only fourteen years of marriage. Matthew was 51 when he died in 1820. But these fourteen years produced five children (a biography of Robert Park's brother Patric says six – perhaps one died in infancy?). These were Catherine, named for her maternal grandmother (1807), Agnes, named for her paternal grandmother (1810), Patric, who adopted the old Scottish spelling of his paternal grandfather Patrick's name (1811), Robert for his maternal grandfather (1812), and Elizabeth, (1816).

The family first lived in Gallowgate, probably in a tenement dwelling. 'Tenement' is a legal term for a piece of land, but the word now conjures up a picture of the most sordid slums. In Grandfather Patrick's, Father Matthew's and even in the Park children's day, it wasn't so. Tenements might be substantial apartments 'of fine rooms' (even, at the turn of the 18th to 19th century, with indoor water closets). The Burgess class lived in these apartments, often set in gardens. On the side facing the road and opening on to it would be the merchant or guild brother's place of business, the family home on the floor or floors above. It was only later with the rapid growth in Glasgow's population that radical infilling happened and the later 19th and early 20th century slums were created. The year Robert (or Bob) was born on 7 January 1812 the family were in King Street, and then for a year or so in Virginia Street. From 1816 to when Matthew died on 17 July 1820, they lived in these apartments.

The City of Glasgow in the early 19th century. The streets coloured yellow are where the Parks lived or had property at some time. John Street is where the Grammar School was when Robert attended.

It was a well-found family. Matthew had increased the goodly inheritance from his father Patrick, and now Matthew's widow Catherine and her five children were left comfortably off. The sum of £1249 -14s -5d was owed by various debtors to Matthew's estate. There was an interest in property, some shared with his brother and sister, by his father Patrick's 1803 Deed of Settlement. This property was land and tenements in the village of Gorbals. Matthew had more land in Gorbals, and tenements, Selkriggs and

'Four steadings etc delineated on a plan made out by William Kyle land surveyor'. New tenements (presumably built by Matthew) were at the foot of Stockwell Street near the Old Bridge. It may have been in these new tenements they were living, handy to the 'yards' Matthew owned on Bridgegate where he had also built a new tenement. The value of these properties must have been considerable. His wife Catherine was a trustee of the estate, and was given a life interest in their home. She was to have the 'whole household furniture and plenishings during all the days and years of her lifetime'; Matthew's books, engravings, pictures and 'small museum' were to be taken care of by his spouse. What did he collect? Where did these artifacts go when the family moved to London in the 1830s? That will probably remain unknown.

But here in 1821 were two boys (aged 8 and 9) to be educated. Glasgow Grammar School beckoned for the nearly 10-year-old Patric, and hard on his heels, Robert. In 1821 the school had migrated from the 1460 site behind High Street to George Street and then to John Street. The buildings are now gone. Both boys were at Grammar School until they were 14, when it was their turn to serve an apprenticeship. The grammar curriculum had expanded from classical specialities to include English, Mathematics, Chemistry etc., and this was to serve young Bob, in particular, very well.

'East view of the Bridgegate from Stockwell.'
The Parks were in Stockwell when Matthew Park died in 1820.

Vol. I Glasgow Ancient and Modern. James Cleland Glasgow 1840.

Patric Park has sketched himself in the studio in Rome where he studied sculpture under Thorvaldsen. In 1833, it is said, Patric Park had completed an important statue which he discovered, had in the night, been accidentally destroyed before his master Thorvaldsen could see it. Patric 'the most impulsive of men – at once locked his studio door, quitted Rome, and returned to his native country'.

Drawing and Prints A-215-013 A.T.L.

His older brother Patric had had an excellent start. He had shown talent as an architectural mason when apprenticed to John Connell who was building Hamilton Palace. With his gift for stone carving recognised it led to his becoming a renowned portrait sculptor, executing works for many of the rich and famous of the day, among them the Dukes of Hamilton, Newcastle and Sutherland, Sir Charles Napier and Charles Dickens. He also sculpted historical figures such as Robert Burns and Oliver Cromwell.

Young Bob was apprenticed in February 1827 to William Kyle, a Glasgow land surveyor who had done much work for his builder father, Matthew. He was with him seven years until February 1834 and it seems was still living at home with his mother and sisters in Glasgow.

A chalk self portrait of Patric Park in 1834 which he has titled 'The Devil'. The narrow face belies a man of 'powerful frame'. Brother Bob was of the same build.

Courtesy of the Inverness Courier.
Held by the National Library of Scotland.

In 1833 brother Patric came back to Britain after two years in Rome, where, by the patronage of the Duke of Hamilton, he had studied sculpture with the famed Berkel Thorvaldsen. Patric lived two years in Edinburgh before going to London in 1835, to Euston Square, where he had a studio.

Bob, meanwhile, had finished his apprenticeship with William Kyle. He had fulfilled his obligations in his contract of seven years 'in a manner highly creditable to himself and satisfactory to me'. His indentures had stipulated that he work '9½ hours each lawful day … and further attendance if required'. He was allowed one week for 'recreation' in each year, at 'such time as suited his master'. He received wages of £11-14-0 in his first year, £62-8-0 in his last. Not bad, when it is considered that a surveyor's apprentice had often to pay a fee to his master surveyor when taken on. William Kyle also wrote 'that he had laid down surveys with accuracy and uncommon dispatch, his genius in drawing is very superior'. Robert had been regular in attendance and 'his whole conduct towards me has been such as to render him fully entitled to my best wishes for his prosperity in every respect', Kyle concluded.

With this excellent testimonial in hand, Robert found work in 1834 as an engineer with the Paisley Water Works, and then was employed on the Glasgow to Edinburgh railway survey where he received a further flattering testimonial. This latter experience led to his being employed on the Great Western Railway. The renowned Isambard Brunel was the Chief Engineer, appointed in 1833. Brunel had, it was said, surveyed

Church of St Mary Redcliffe Bristol, where Robert Park married Mary Anne Morgan on 6 August 1837.

Photo Heather Murchison.

the entire length of the railway himself, from London to Bristol.

But engineer Gavatt (known for an improved version of the dumpy level called the Gavatt Level) would be Robert Park's immediate superior when he worked on the extension of the Great Western from Bristol to Exeter. He was not however, to be at its opening, nor even of the London to Bristol line in 1841.

Robert had become enthusiastic at the prospect of working with the Wakefields and the New Zealand Company having learned of their colonising proposals for New Zealand. While working in Bristol he had met, and on 6 August 1837 married, Mary Anne Morgan in the church of St Mary Redcliffe. Ten months later on 16 June

Mary Anne Park's
mother Jane Martha
Morgan (née Perry).

Courtesy Stewart Robinson.

'Little Kate'. This sculpted portrait of Catherine Park is with a descendant of Mary Anne and Robert Park in Australia. It may have come with Mary Anne to New Zealand on the *Aurora* in 1840. It is said to have survived an earthquake in Wellington, most probably that of late 1848.

Courtesy Bruce Robinson.

1838, Catherine Park was born at the small town of Bampton in Devon, not too far from the route of the Bristol to Exeter rail which Park was prospecting. 'Little Kate' was the darling of her paternal grandmother Catherine, for whom she was named, and of her uncle Patric, and her aunts Catherine, Agnes and Eliza. By 1838 all the Park family apart from Robert were in London, which would be his mother and sisters' home to the end of their days.

A year on from Little Kate's birth, Robert received an appointment on 8 July 1839 as assistant surveyor to the New Zealand Company. He had had recommendations from a number of names to whom no doubt he had respectfully applied. To another 'flattering' testimonial from Isambard Brunel, and those from Kyle and the Paisley Water Works, were added the approving support of the Duke of Sutherland (for whom Patric Park was to do a sculpture), Sir George Sinclair, Sir J. Guest and others.

On 1 August 1839 Robert sailed from Gravesend on the *Cuba*, leaving a very pregnant Mary Anne to follow a little later, as this small ship could only accommodate those essential to the setting up of the first settlement. Mary Anne sailed on the *Aurora* on 22 September, some seven weeks after Robert. She was accompanied by her sister,

The Bristol & Exeter Railway

'Twas on November the first day
That we began this great Survey
Which splendid genius doth display
The Bristol & Exeter Railway

Brunel he was Chief Engineer
Grovatt the skilful Pioneer
Who taught us still the way to steer
And make the noble line appear
No heart forget him ever shall
He was so kind unto us all
Never a harsh word let he fall
On the Bristol & Exeter Railway.
Chorus
With our chains and poles and levelling rods
Theodolites Level & then tri.-pods
And all the other ends and odds
On the Bristol & Exeter Railway.

'Twould be in vain for me to say
Of all who met on this survey
'Twould take me more than half a day
On the Bristol & Exeter Railway
But there was Harry Beetham bright
I cannot pass him over quite
He all the ladies hearts did smite
He was such a splendid Ex-quisite
He was Corinthian – thorough bred
With his carroty whiskers all so red
His silken vest & shaven head
On the Bristol & Exeter Railway
Chorus
With our chains …

Bridgewater Williams too did shine
With his peacock voice all-most divine
And those raven locks so very fine
On the Bristol & Exeter Railway
Oh when we met at night to dine
Our jaded carcuses to line
Perfumed with smoke & wet with wine
Lord! how cigars & wit did shine
With gallant Bingley in the chair
And Baker with his Irish air
Who banished every thing like care
From the Bristol & Exeter Railway.
Chorus
With our chains …

The lawyers too were men of skill
And did their business with a will
That no flaw might be in the Bill
For the Bristol & Exeter Railway
On Monday night when all was oér
And the last carriage left the door
Bridgewater never heard before
Such a long wild & deaf'ning roar
In rattling cars away they flew
The plans were lodged as ye may view
And may we all soon meet anew
On the Bristol & Exeter Railway
Chorus
With our chains …

Robert Park ca 1838.

It's oh to be married & never to rue
To have plenty of money and nothing to do
Live like a Prince & banish all care
With a charming young creature my pleasure to share

All the day long we would sail o'er the sea
All the night long we would drink merrily
With my wife & my glass & havannah cigar
I'd defy all the world my pleasure to mar.

If blessed with a dear little girl or boy
We'd teach them the way to cultivate joy
In mirth, in good humour, in frolic & fun
To live as there jolly old parents had done.

We'd ne'er be so foolish as send them [to] school
Where they'd learn nonsense & then play the fool
But teach them to steer or handle an oar
And shoot, box or ride when they were ashore

Then its etc.

Robert Park ca 1837.

Poems by Robert Park.

Deans Family Papers Riccarton Bush Trust.

Jane Emily Morgan, who had been a bridesmaid and witness at her sister's marriage to Robert Park. No record has been found of how this young mother of 22 years felt leaving behind Little Kate, now a toddler of 15 months, however loving were her grandmother, uncle and aunts in London. Would she see her child, indeed any of them, again? Would her baby to be born in a months time, survive the voyage? Where in New Zealand was the New Zealand Company Settlement to be? How was Robert faring on the *Cuba*? Where and when would they meet again?

CHAPTER 3

INTRODUCING MUNGO PARK

Mungo Park, the traveller; Mungo Park the explorer in West Africa; his name forever associated with the great Niger River and its source.

Mungo Park, after his journeying in West Africa and the interior, became a good friend of Sir Walter Scott. Sir Walter Scott was Sheriff of Selkirkshire, and at this time lived over the ridge dividing the Yarrow and Tweed valleys.

The beautiful vales of the Yarrow and the Ettrick water were the home ground of Mungo Park. The waters of these rivers combined to join the Tweed which flowed to the north of Selkirk county town on its hill above the Ettrick River. Mungo Park and Sir Walter Scott were both deeply interested in the history of the Borders, and the battles over the debatable land which were waged dur-

The tranquil Vale of Yarrow today.
Photo Heather Murchison.

Ettrick Water on a peaceful July day in 2008.

Photo Heather Murchison.

Mungo Park's old home at Foulshiels on the Yarrow four miles west of the town of Selkirk. Insert is an enlargement of the plaque on the house wall.

Photo Heather Murchison.

ing the Jacobite uprisings, and the earlier bitter Civil Wars of the time of Charles I. Sir Walter Scott wrote a rousing poem of the 'Blue Bonnets'. Here is the chorus:

March! March! Ettrick and Tevot-dale,
Why my lads dinnaye march forward in order
March! March! Eskdale and Liddesdale!
All the blue bonnets are over the border.

Liddesdale, it may be recalled, is where the Glasgow Parks were thought to have originated. The long narrative poems of Scott in the *Minstrelsy of the Scottish Border* told how the Jacobites were urged to 'Fight for your King and the old Scottish Border'. The last battle in the Civil War in this area was fought at Philiphaugh, in the mid 1650s, since when there had been peace here, even when the men of Ettrick and Liddesdale were marching for Bonnie Prince Charlie in 1745, the uprising which culminated in his defeat at Culloden in 1746. Philiphaugh is between Selkirk town and Foulshiels, up the Yarrow valley, the farm where Mungo Park was born in 1771 and grew up. He was seventh in a large family of 12 born to Mungo senior and Elspeth Park. Seven of the family lived to adulthood. Mungo senior was a tenant farmer of the Duke of Buccleuch, comfortably off, and was able to educate his children by private tutor and then at the Grammar School in Selkirk. At 14 Mungo was apprenticed to Dr Anderson of Selkirk who lived and practiced opposite where the memorial to Mungo Park stands today. At 17 Mungo attended Edinburgh University where he studied medicine. But he had always been more interested in travel and botany than doctoring and in 1792 set off for London to begin his adventurous life. On his trip to Sumatra as a surgeon's mate on an East Indiaman, he brought back botanical specimens for Sir Joseph Banks who was a member of the African Association. It was through Banks that Park set off in 1795 for Gambia 'to ascertain the course, and if possible the rise and termination of the river Niger'. Mungo Park was to be away for two years and seven

A detail from an illustration in *Pioneers in West Africa* by Sir Harry Johnston showing Mungo Park's tall black beaver hat in which he stored his diary notes and sketches. At the time he is depicted here, his horse was in fact an unrideable bag of bones and his clothes in shreds.

months. He suffered the most awful privations – of being held prisoner by the Moors, of starvation and of humiliation.

He eventually returned to Selkirk where he wrote an account of his adventures, *Travels in the Interior Districts of Africa. Performed in the Years 1795, 1796 and 1797.* The 1799 publication was a best-seller with three editions in the first year, a fourth in 1800, the sixth in 1810. In the year of his book's publication Mungo married his 'Lovely Allie,' Allison Anderson, daughter of his former doctor employer.

Now, with responsibilities of a wife and then children, he reluctantly practiced as a doctor in Peebles. In 1804, at last, he was invited to go again to West Africa; to go again to the Niger and follow its course as far as it could be traced. It ended in the tragic death of Alexander Anderson, his close friend and brother-in-law, and other companions by illness, and then in Mungo's own end in early 1806, perishing with others of the party, probably by drowning.

An engraving depicting Mungo Park is a frontispiece in the *Travels* published in 1799.

Just before Mungo left Selkirkshire on his last adventure he had ridden out with Sir Walter Scott one misty morning along a ridge between the Tweed and Yarrow valleys. Mungo's horse stumbled and nearly threw him. Scott thought that it might be a bad omen. Mungo quickly quoted an old border proverb. 'Freits follow those who look to them.' But Walter Scott never saw his friend again.

Mungo Park was a contemporary of Robert Park's father, Matthew Park, who was born in 1769. And in the same year that surveyor-to-be Robert Park was born in Glasgow on 7 January 1812, over in Selkirk, Alison, the wife of Mungo Park's brother, Alexander, on 16 October 1812, gave birth to another Robert Park.

The area around the Yarrow and Ettrick Rivers with names both here and in the final chapter, seen in the glass. The relationship of Glasgow and Edinburgh to Selkirk is shown. Culross is where the infant St Mungo grew up and Fulfordlees near the east coast is where Robert Park's family may have come from centuries ago, settling near and in Glasgow from perhaps the 17th century.

Frank Easdale

CHAPTER 4

ARRIVAL IN NEW ZEALAND 1839-1841

J ust before Christmas in 1839 the *Cuba* nosed into the Kaipara Harbour on the northern west coast of New Zealand.

She was looking for the ship *Tory* with Colonel William Wakefield aboard, on his mission of land purchase for the New Zealand Company. *Tory* was missed as she lay hidden around the headland, and the Captain of the *Cuba*, rightly apprehensive that she might go aground on the numerous shoals, determined to sail on to D'Urville Island and Port Hardy at the top of Marlborough Sounds in the South Island. Those on the *Cuba* still didn't know where the first New Zealand Company settlement was to be.

The *Cuba* with its complement of surveyors – Captain Mein Smith (Surveyor General), Wellington Carrington (Principal Assistant Surveyor), and Assistant Surveyors Robert Park and Robert Stokes, with 21 labouring assistants, had had a slow passage from England. At Cape Verde Islands, the *Cuba* had nearly gone on the rocks after dragging her anchor in a storm. She stood off for four days, then returned to pick up a shore party. This party brought the deadly yellow fever aboard. Two passengers died. Robert Park fell seriously ill. The doctor had 'given up' on Robert, but this robust man recovered.

After watering and wooding at Port Hardy, the *Cuba* sailed north across Cook Strait to massive Kapiti Island, the favoured, sheltered port of call for vessels on that open and dangerous west coast, and also a haven for whalers.

At Kapiti they learned that Port Nicholson had been purchased on 27 September and was to be the site of the Company's principal settlement. Captain Young, a whaler, piloted the *Cuba* around into Port Nicholson harbour, where she dropped anchor on 4 January 1840. Now began a busy time on Petone Beach, in preparation for the arrival of the immigrant ships. Maori helped with the building of huts and temporary shelter. These were Te Atiawa from the Taranaki region who were in possession of the Petone foreshore not, as the Company agents supposed, the whole of the Hutt Valley – this was Ngati Toa land. This 'misunderstanding' would lead to the building of forts and fighting in a few years. A wharf was run out, but the surveys of the purchase did not begin until a few days before the first immigrant ship, the *Aurora*, arrived on 22 January 1840. It brought Robert Park's dear young wife Mary Anne, and in her arms three and a half months old Robert Wakefield, born fewer than six weeks after the *Aurora* had sailed from London.

Aboard also were a Scot, William Deans, and Major Baker. Both would play a part in the Park story. The voyage of the *Aurora* had been smooth and swift. One child had died but there had been four births. The vessel had not seen land since leaving Dover, wrote home one immigrant, until 'a dark cloud' on the horizon was seen – New Zealand. On the whole they had lived well, wrote another, and there was dancing on the deck every fine night. Perhaps on those starry nights at sea romance blossomed, and Mary Anne's sister, Jane Emily, and the dashing Major fell in love. William Deans writes of Baker as 'a most gentlemanly young man'. Baker would fight a gentlemanly duel on arrival at Petone, with Deans acting as his second.

The collection of tents and huts on the Petone Beach did not become the principal settlement, although it was given the grand name of 'Britannia' at the end of March. The land behind the beach was swampy and the Hutt River in March flooded the hopeful steadings of some settlers who had penetrated the dense Hutt forests, and again in May and June. But by June the embryo town of Wellington (a contentious alternative site) had largely been surveyed.

Robert Park had gone to Thorndon on 8 April, and begun the subdivision of town acres on the 10th. But resident Maori pulled up the pegs and halted the work. It had been sold to the Company, they contended, by people who were not the acknowledged owners of the land. In the end, with the promise that no land claimed by that tribe would be sold to settlers, that their claim would be looked into by the commissioners, and that they would be dealt with fairly, the survey went ahead on 14 April. Maori politics concerned with land were ill understood by the Company and its surveyors. Park's answer to the stopping of the survey had been to obtain 17 cutlasses and 17 pistols perhaps as a show of strength against possible conflict.

Though Jerningham Wakefield called Mein Smith 'a great dawdle', the hard-pressed Company's Surveyor General, despite being understaffed and badly accommodated in an ill-lit, leaky whare managed to have plans ready for inspection by 25 July. Sections were allotted in the main to the immigrants who had purchased their town and country sections back in England. Some were absentee owners. One was the Duke of Sutherland, a sponsor of Robert Park. He would assist Robert again in the future. A selection was made a week or so later and within a fortnight houses and business premises were being erected.

William Deans had been enlisted as a foreman of a team on the surveys back in Petone. The team cut the lines which the surveyors had laid out. He considered himself to be fortunate to be employed (at £20 per 100 chains) and was grateful to Robert Park. 'This (the line cutting) was spoken of to me by Mr. Park, one of the surveyors, a brother of the sculptor, with whom I am acquainted. The way it is done is – Captain Smith or one of his assistants lays out with the theodolite a line which requires to be cut straight, and this you are obliged to do, altho' you should meet trees 50 feet in circumference.' Down came the trees. He liked the work.

William Deans went with Robert Park, his colleague Robert Stokes, Charles Heaphy, New Zealand Company artist, surveyor and draughtsman, and Jerningham Wakefield. Six men assisted with baggage and provisions on an extended overland journey as far as Taranaki, 'to examine the practicability of a good land communication from Wellington to Wanganui and determine the best areas for country sections to be surveyed'. A full account of the journey written by Robert Stokes appeared in the *New Zealand Gazette* newspaper over three weeks beginning on 7 November 1840.

The party set off from Wellington through hilly terrain to Porirua Harbour where they stayed at Captain Daniell's whaling station (a transient venture), then climbed over the hill to Pukerua Bay and followed the rocky foreshore to reach Waikanae where the Rev. Octavius Hadfield had his Anglican Mission, on Te Atiawa territory. They stayed the night. Not far away was Otaki, the domain of Ngati Toa and the Chief Rauparaha. Stokes judged there was about 20, 000 acres of flat land hereabouts and remarked, nostalgically, that where Maori had cleared land, this, with the sombre treed background, had 'almost the appearance of a bit of English landscape transported to the foot of the New Zealand Hills'.

Relations with Maori at the kainga were amiable, until a quantity of tobacco, three shot belts and other articles were taken. When the people were threatened with giving the place a bad name on the party's return to Port Nicholson, pretty well everything was restored. But a demand for utu for their return was refused. Robert Park thought this propensity for theft among Maori should be severely dealt with.

They reached at length the Manawatu River. Here there was a fishing pā. Great posts of totara with which the banks were strewn by floods, were used for the posts. They learned here that the Manawatu River had its rise in Ngati Kahungunu territory on the east coast, a journey of some six days in canoe and a further five days on foot.

They travelled on to the Rangitikei River, broad and rapid but not deep. They viewed between the Manawatu and Rangitikei Rivers, the most level and extensive district they had yet seen, and saw in the extreme distance Tongariro rearing 'his massive head and extended sides covered with snow'. Further on they glimpsed Mount Egmont (Taranaki), then crossed the broad, shallow but swift Turakina River. Here and at the Whangaehu, which had its rise on Mount Tongariro, the water was very cold.

It was not far then to the hill looking down to the Whanganui River. Here they found missionaries Mason and Matthews on opposite banks of the river. But the surveyors stayed in the substantial 60 x 30 foot house which the Chief E Kuru had built for Wakefield's return. Maori had been waiting for settlers and other houses had also been built in anticipation.

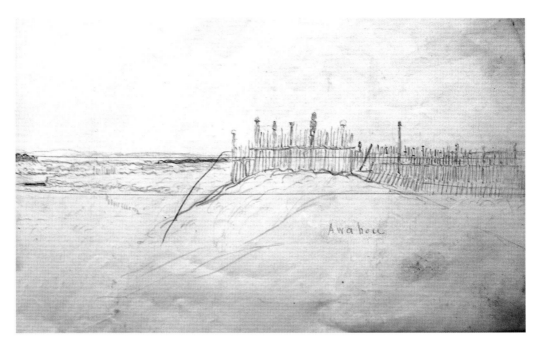

Pā at Awahou north of the Manawatu River which became the site of the present day Foxton.
R Park FB 72 LINZ Wellington.

Park spent three days surveying and sounding the Whanganui from its mouth to 'Kau Warapaoa' a pā next to a stream of that name; about 24 miles. E Kuru was coiled up in the bow of the canoe giving them the names of every settlement and tributary, which Park noted on his plan. 'Mr. Park has made a careful drawing of it, as well as of the line of coast we traversed, and if compared with the published will add much to our previous information', wrote Stokes. A plan now lost, it appears.

Wakefield stayed at Wanganui, while Park, Stokes and Deans journeyed on to Taranaki, which would be the site of the future New Plymouth settlement. They did not move north from here to Waitara as planned. Provisions were hard to come by. All the talk by Maori at Nga Motu had been of the arrival of immigrants, and their energies had been directed to building accommodation for them rather than cultivation of food. The exploring party slept in a house 140 feet x 18 feet with seven doors and a verandah and there were two more going up, 90 feet each in length, as immigrant barracks. On 27 September they left Nga Motu. Six days later they were back at Patea. From here they took an inland route back to Wanganui – another two days.

Park and Deans set out by boat from Wanganui to return to Wellington. A note in the *New Zealand Gazette* of 17 October 1840 records the arrival of the ship *Magnet* with 'Messrs Park and Deans, on board, who were driven to sea in a boat from Wanganui, and fortunately picked up by this vessel'. This story became exaggerated in time to how they had been swept out to sea in a raging storm and would have lost their lives had not the *Magnet* picked them up. Don't believe it, William Deans wrote to his father, it is just the newspaper's mistake. Yes, there was a storm and 'although in a gale of wind for three days and three nights we got safe to Kapiti'. Of course *Magnet* had called at sheltered Kapiti Island as usual and picked up overseas mail from the *Lavinia* from New South Wales which was returning to Sydney. From Kapiti the two men took passage on the *Magnet* to Port Nicholson.

With Stokes' lengthy report to the Company was a map of the coast from the Sugar Loaf Islands to Port Nicholson, 'prepared by Mr. Park far different from that which had been published by the Admiralty or Mr. M'Donnel of Hokianga. The most striking difference is that in Mr. Park's which may be relied on, there is not even the slightest appearance of what had been termed Taranaki Bay. It is impossible to look at this map and not feel this [Port Nicholson] is the harbour of the Straits.' When back in Wellington Park drew up a plan of Wanganui (then named Petre) town sections. Mein Smith wrote of this plan when he sent off a report on the journey. It would not be Park however who pegged out the lots, but Wellington Carrington and his assistants. Park authenticated in 1850 the original plan of Wanganui township when he wrote a note on a copy of the plan he had drawn in 1840, certifying it as a 'true copy'. The first 100 town sections were ready for selection in March 1841. But by that time Park was no longer employed by the New Zealand Company, although he continued to do contract work for the Company.

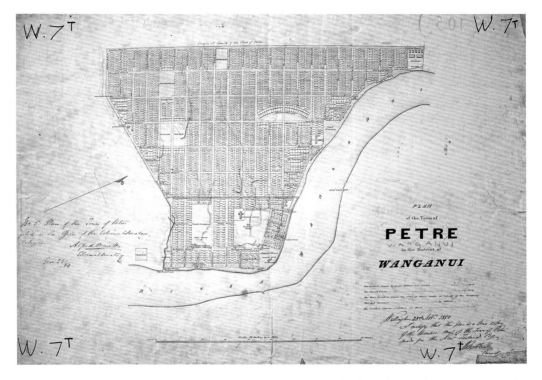

Plan of the town of Petre in the District of Wanganui 1850. Certified by Robert Park as a true copy of the 1840 plan.

(AAFV997,W7T) Archives New Zealand/Te Rua Mahara o te Kawanatanga Wellington Office.

Mary Anne and her sister Jane Emily were still at Petone when Robert returned in October. They had sad news to give the father of baby Robert Wakefield. With what satisfaction had Robert seen his son christened on 24 May by the Rev. J. Churton, and the event entered in the Church of England baptismal register. Now in the Church of England burial register Robert Wakefield's name was entered. His was the third child death since settlement began. The baby had died on 1 September and was laid to rest, nobody knows exactly where now, in the newly surveyed Bolton Street cemetery.

He was 10 months old. Only three weeks after this tragic event, some Maori had entered the Park dwelling, alarming the women who were alone. Wrote Ensign Best: 'Some natives went to Mr. Parke's [sic] home and a servant maid bringing out a cutlass to intimidate them it was wrested from her and her hand was severely cut. The Natives, alarmed at what they had done escaped into the bush.' (Was this one of the cutlasses that Park had obtained in the April previously?) How glad they must have been to have Robert in the house again with them, even though he was backwards and forwards on the Wellington survey. There was no road along the foreshore between Wellington and Petone then and travel was by boat.

To cheer Robert there was the jollity of celebrating St Andrew's Day on 30 November. Robert Park acted as a 'croupier' (a vice-chairman at a dinner table in this sense) at one table supported by gentlemen on each side. Toast followed toast. First the Queen with three times three 'and one cheer more' for the expected baby Prince of Wales; to members of the Royal Family; to 'Her Majesty's Ministers, reformation to them, and a speedy enlightenment of their views with regard to New Zealand'. They, the New Zealand. Company settlers, had been deserted like foundlings, and they felt the Government in London would benefit by 'an addition to their optical sense'. To Governor Hobson, as representative of this Government. They were anxious to see him and show him what kind of people the Port Nicholson people were. And to challenge him as to 'whether it was right that labour which had been imported into the Colony at the expense of the Company should be taken away by Government?'. Hear, hear cheered the assembly, and with this 'sole exception' to the toast, it was drunk with warmest wishes. Then – the Army and Navy – and the greatest hero, the Duke of Wellington, whose name their town bore. 'Rule Britannia' was sung.

Then to toasts to touch their heart strings – to Scotland. Robert Park proposed a toast to the memory of St Andrew. A man he never saw in his life. He supposed though 'that as he was a Scotsman, he must have been a good man'. (Robert was a proud Scot and favoured fellow Scots above others in his dealings – he firmly believed, they were better, braver, more intelligent and practical than the general run of men.) On went more toasts – one by J.C. Crawford, a friend of Robert Park. Crawford related that when he first came from Australia to Port Nicholson, he had found only one European man, (a Mr. Robinson). Now after a trip to Sydney to get cattle, he had returned to find 'an embryo city, a bank, a church, and all the ramifications of a civilised society'. A toast therefore, to the agent Colonel William Wakefield and the New Zealand Company. Robert Strang toasted the newly arrived Rev J. McFarlane of the Kirk of Scotland (for whom a Scotch church was yet to be built). And then came the turn of 'Captain Smith and the officers of the Surveying Department', with Robert Park acknowledging the toast. And so it went on, and on, with Scotland's 'two brightest luminaries' Robbie Burns

Major Richard Baker. R. Park.
Courtesy David Deans Estate.

and Sir Walter Scott and their 'poesy and romance' of that land being loudly and nostalgically toasted.

Glasses were no doubt raised again following another happy event – the wedding of Mary Anne Park's sister Jane Emily Morgan to Major Richard Baker on Christmas Eve, 24 December 1840. Robert Park and Colonel William Wakefield were witnesses. Colonel Wakefield appropriately, as Baker had been with him in the British Legion in Spain a few years prior to 1840.

Colonel Wakefield was the Principal Agent for the New Zealand Company, and it was to him that Captain Mein Smith had applied when Robert Park and Robert Stokes wrote to Smith to request an increase in their salaries from £150 p.a. Wakefield authorised a further £50 p.a. On the 30 December 1840 Robert wrote to Smith to say he was not satisfied with £200 p.a. and 'that unless the Company's Principal

Agent would guarantee £300 a year for the next year exclusive of ration money the year commencing from the 7 July last' he should be obliged to tender his resignation. The Colonel couldn't or wouldn't and Park ceased to be employed by the Company on 7 January 1841. Mein Smith could ill afford to lose his assistant surveyor, even if he had on occasion been 'obliged to pull up Mr Park for swearing'. He was 'a very good fellow' but was 'loud, boisterous and a great swearer'. This is when Park went into private practice, doing some New Zealand Company work under contract.

Aglionby Arms. The Hutt River flooded settlers buildings many times. This Park sketch shows the severe listing of the Aglionby Arms undermined by flood waters. ca. 1842.

Drawings and Prints A.T.L. A-032-024.

CHAPTER 5

LIFE IN WELLINGTON 1841-1845

There were to be celebrations in January 1841 to commemorate the first anniversary of the arrival of the first immigrant ship, the *Aurora*.

There was to be a regatta, horse racing, a rifle match and a ball at Barretts Hotel on the Quay. It is probable that Robert Park, Richard Baker and their ladies were included in the 'most respectable' 80 to 90 guests at the ball. 22 January was a stormy day and although the races and regatta were postponed, the ladies were taken to Barretts in a tilt waggon (an army ammunition waggon) drawn by four bullocks. They danced the night away to a band of piano, violin and flute and at dawn, at 5a.m., under cleared skies, they walked (danced?) their way home.

For hearts that were perhaps beginning to lighten after the sadness of the previous year, it must have been dreadful for Robert and Mary Anne to receive

Wellington gents.
R Park FB 54 LINZ Wellington.

a letter from England telling of the death of Little Kate, their first child. Was it from brother Patric, or sister Catherine who was with her when she died, aged 2 years

The 1839 sculpted portrait of 'Little Kate' (on page 18) would be cold comfort in its marble stillness in 1842, to grieving parents. This 1840 Patric Park sculpture is inscribed 'ONE WHOM THE GODS LOVED'. It had stood in the Sefton Park Palm House in Liverpool but was removed when this was refurbished. Stolen in 1966, it was found in 1989, damaged and badly repaired at a London art dealers. It is at present on loan to Liverpool Women's Hospital. Now that the child's name, history and her sad death in the year it was sculpted are known, Nigel Sharp, Parks and Development Officer, hopes it will be seen once more in the lavishly planted Palm House.

Photo Nigel Sharp, Liverpool City Council.

and 4 months, on 29 October 1840 (of a bowel complaint her death certificate informs). She died at the house where Patric had his studio at George Street, Euston Square, London.

Kate had been christened just months before at Old Church St Pancras, near to where Patric's mother and sisters lived. She was laid to rest in the Kensal Green Cemetery, where her aunts and grandmother in time would lie with her. It is poignant to realise that the two Park children had died within two months of each other, the grieving relatives at the opposite ends of the earth not knowing for many months of the other child's passing.

Mary Anne could have been pregnant again when the English letter finally came. On 1 January 1842 at Park Cottage, Wellington, a daughter was born. When they had built there or moved from Petone to Wellington is not known. Robert had purchased part of Captain Daniells' section (Daniells had erected a pre-fab house at Te Aro flat) and added it to part of another lot bought from Francis Wilson. Although his address was The Terrace (as it is now known) in fact the property ran through from

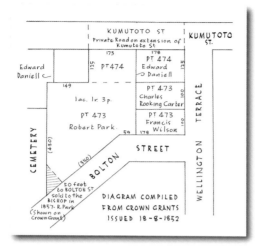

Park Cottage site in Wellington built on by 1842.

Frank Easdale

Bolton Street to Kumutoto Street (now Bowen Street which continues beyond the old end of Kumutoto Street). Over the fence to the west was the Bolton Street Cemetery. Kumutoto Stream ran through these sections to Kumutoto Pā. Near here the Chief Wiremu Tako Ngatata lived. He had inherited in 1842 the mantle of Wharepouri, an ariki of Port Nicholson and one who had been a signatory to the sale of land to the New Zealand Company. The handsome Wi Tako Ngatata would be important, not only to Wellington as it grew but as a close relative of the Maori inheritors of the Park name.

An article to attract more immigrants appeared in the *New Zealand Journal*, the mouthpiece of the New Zealand Company which was published in England. This meant more land needed to be subdivided in anticipation of an influx. 1842 saw a major subdivision designed by Park advertised in the *New Zealand Gazette and Wellington Spectator*. The proposed new town of Te Maire stretched from Lake Horowhenua on the Manawatu Plains to the south bank of the Manawatu, and extended up the river almost to the present Massey University outside Palmerston North. Park, after all, had had practice designing Wanganui township. Te Maire was going to rival Wanganui. Nothing, however, came of this grand plan. The land purchase by the New Zealand Company was in dispute, and instead of the 25,000 acres they alleged they had purchased, Commissioner Spain awarded 900 acres. Some immigrants settled up the river, but in the later conflicts of 1846, fear of the Chief Rangihaeata, whose last stronghold was nearby, caused them to leave. Some would never return. The towns of Shannon and Levin are on the edges of this ambitious plan.

Park, however, seems to have been attracting other work, mainly for Wellington people. Would he have earned more had he stayed in the Company's employ? Mein Smith had been displaced as Surveyor General by the arrival of Samuel Brees in February 1842, forcing him to set up, as had Park, in private practice. Brees was to have five assistant surveyors each employed at £200 p.a, the salary Park had been offered, though with expenses to cover horses and field equipment. This in the '42–'43 year, not too bad? But Park was to get a boost to his income. Indeed, although there had been

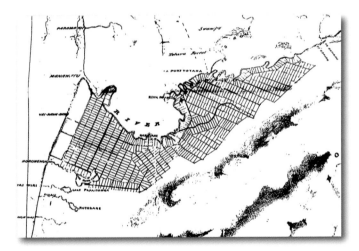

Part of a 'Map of the first Settlement of the New Zealand Company shewing Port Nicholson, Manawatu and Wanganui August 1842'.

AAFV997 WII3T, Archives New Zealand. Te Rua Mahara o te Kawanatanga Wellington Office.

Right: Te Maire – The advertisement from the *New Zealand Gazette and Wellington Spectator* explains the plan.

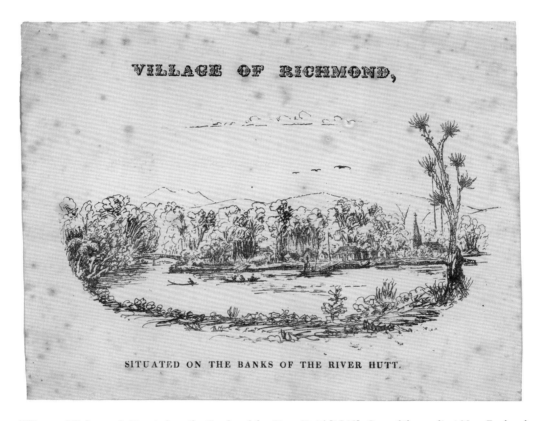

VILLAGE OF RICHMOND,

SITUATED ON THE BANKS OF THE RIVER HUTT.

'Village of Richmond, Situated on the Banks of the River Hutt' [1842]. One of the earliest New Zealand lithographs, executed in Wellington by Robert Park.

Drawings and Prints A-215-004 A.T.L.

no written application, in October 1842 the Wellington Municipal Council agreed it was important to appoint a Town Surveyor, and 'it was generally understood that Robert Park, Esq., would not decline the appointment'. Of course he didn't and would do the first year at the nominal sum of £50 per annum. Later he would receive double this as well as some perks, and it added to his income from private practice.

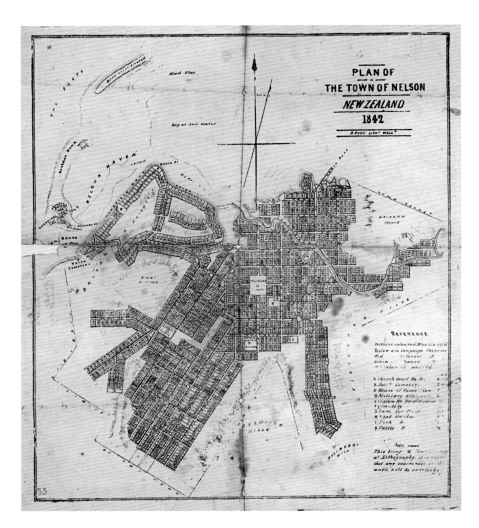

'Plan of the Town of Nelson New Zealand 1842'. It is probable that the plan of the New Zealand Company Settlement of Nelson lithographed by Park in 1842 was produced at the same time as that of the Village of Richmond. Park notes on the plan 'This being the first attempt at Lithography it is expected that any coarseness in the work will be overlooked'.

M53 Bett Collection Nelson Provincial Museum.

An advertisement for the purchase of copies appeared in the *New Zealand Colonist* on 2 August 1842.

Two important works of Robert Park were displayed in Wellington in 1842. These were among the first lithographs to be executed in Wellington. One was a charming depiction of the 'Town of Richmond' on the Hutt River. The other was of the new New Zealand Company settlement at Nelson, where by March 1842 surveyors had laid out the town lots. Park adds a note to the plan. 'This being a first attempt at Lithography it is expected, that any coarseness in the work will be overlooked.' An advertisement appeared in the *New Zealand Colonist and Port Nicholson Advertiser* on 1 August 1842 for copies for purchase of a 'Just Published' plan of the Nelson Settlement. However the advertisement was also for a Chaffers Chart of Cook Straits, from England. Don't buy it, fumed several outraged surveyors and merchants in a notice a fortnight later in the *Gazette* – 'the chart may be compiled from several authentic surveys of harbours, but intervening parts of the coastline is erroneous, … rendering the whole not only useless, but pernicious.'

Why did an advertisement for the sale of Park Cottage appear in the *New Zealand Gazette and Wellington Spectator* a year after Mary Jane Park had been born there? Mary Anne Park, her mother, was expecting again, and it is said, wrote grandmother Martha Morgan in England, that she wanted to go home, so apprehensive had she become. And perhaps, too, Robert was not doing as well as he had hoped? In the event they didn't sell and on 6 June 1843 another daughter, Agnes, was born to 'The lady of R. Park Esq.'. On that same day, a son was born to Mary Anne Park's sister Emily Baker. Sadly the little fellow later died of convulsions. This loss of her little nephew came not long after word of the Wairau Affray had reached Wellington in July. The tragic event so alarmed the people of Wellington that a military subcommittee was set up of the old hands – Captains Daniell and Mein Smith and Major Baker, who gave

Wellington ca 1845. The view painted by Robert Park is of Colonel Wakefield's house and the Anglican Church not far from his home.

Drawings and Prints A-090-007 A.T.L.

Robert Park the task of organising a defence force against the possibility of invasion. A letter was sent with dozens of signatures expressing the condolences of Wellington people and offering support to those of the Nelson settlement where New Zealand Company relatives, colleagues and friends had died at Tuamarina (near Blenheim).

(An interesting side light. Captain Arthur Wakefield was killed at Tuamarina. He was originally to have headed the New Zealand Company's first venture. Instead he was called to further naval service and only came to New Zealand to be an agent when the Nelson Settlement was founded. He had been with the Navy in the African Mission when Thomas Park, Mungo Park's second son, had gone out to West Africa in 1827 to search for news of his father who, it was assumed, had died there in early 1806. Thomas assisted in aiding explorers to travel inland while there but he was himself to die 140 miles inland on 31 October 1827.)

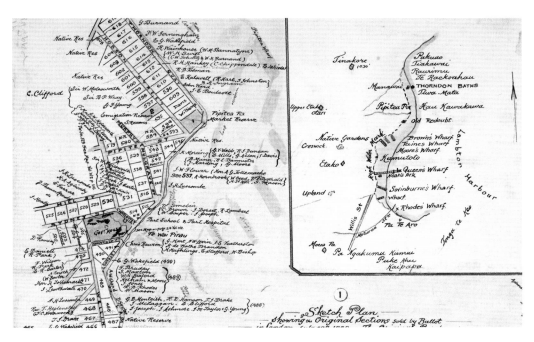

Details from part of a sketch plan of Wellington compiled by Louis Ward from T.H. Fitzgerald's plan of 1840. [1840/1916]

Map Coll. 832.4799gbbd A.T.L.

Part 3 of a lithograph ca 1890 from a panorama drawn by Luke Nattrass in 1841. The cottage identified as no. 48 (bottom) is Wi Tako Ngatata's European-style house, which would become the police station. The house is near the Kumutoto Pā. Wi Tako moved from here to Ngauranga following the 1848 earthquake.

C-029-004-3-2 Drawings and Prints A.T.L.

Although the news that the members of Rauparaha's tribe who had taken part in the affray were back at Otaki gave relief to the anxious settlers, many talked of revenge for the 'massacre'. Alarm at the thought of an invasion of Wellington eventually calmed, and although there was a meeting in October about erecting a monument to commemorate the Wairau men, the idea was dropped due to poor attendance. September had seen a revival of spirits. It was thought good fun (by ladies) to storm somebody's house after church. A jolly party of twenty arrived at Emily Baker's, the home of Mary Anne Park's sister, one Sunday morning, 'in we went … we had great fun' recorded Mary Petre in her journal. 1844 seems to have started off a calmer year but in February 1844 Park Cottage was for sale again. It would seem the nervous Mary Anne still yearned to go home. Robert appears to be complying with her wishes, but he was very much of the Wellington social scene and was also on the Burgess Roll for 1843-44. The cottage wasn't sold. Indeed it was still in Park ownership when Robert died in 1870.

Although there were still thoughts of returning to England, an opportunity arose for the survey of the land proposed for the Free Church of Scotland settlement of New Edinburgh. Frederick Tuckett, the Nelson Principal Surveyor who headed the exploratory survey party south, examined possible sites from Canterbury, through Otago and on to Oreti (future Invercargill) and Stewart Island. The party returned to Otakou Harbour in time for the arrival of the *Deborah* on 15 June 1844 with Robert Park aboard. He had come with the official party of J. J. Symonds, Government Representative, George Clarke Jnr, Sub Protector of the Aborigines, Daniel Wakefield, New Zealand Company and Commissioner Spain. There may have been some thought of Park taking over from Tuckett who fell out with J. J. Symonds who then returned from Otago to Wellington. Two survey cadets, Nicholson and Allom, arrived on the *Carbon* on the17th. On 19 June the survey party set off to survey the boundaries of the proposed Otago purchase. But back in Port Chalmers Tuckett again fell out with the returned J. J. Symonds who, with his friend Daniel Wakefield, sailed once more for Wellington. While they were away Tuckett managed to negotiate with the chiefs for the sale of the block, in a memo signed on 20 June. The sale, he promised the chiefs, would be settled in a months time. The balance of the official party then returned to Wellington on 29 June.

In the meantime Park and the surveyors had set off for the Molyneux (Clutha) River, the southern boundary of the proposed purchase. An excerpt from Park's diary (now destroyed but quoted from by his son Robert George Park) records this uncomfortable foray: '*Wed 24 arrived at river (Molyneux) cannot get across . . . walk back again nothing to eat cannot lie down – too cold – go on – all night again – pushing through gulleys [sic] – climbing precipices tumbling over rocks. Thurs 25 Got to our blankets about 9 am had a short sleep off again reached Taieri river 4 oç – good tuck in – got to bed. Have walked 52 hours distance 80 or 70 miles equal to 100 at home.*'

An advertisement in the *New Zealand Gazette* for the 'Kai Warra Warra Estate'.

On 15 July the *Deborah* was back again from Wellington this time with Colonel William Wakefield accompanying J. J. Symonds. The officials perambulated the block over a week, but viewed the Molyneux only from a good distance. A plan of the Otago Block at a scale of two miles to the inch was drawn with reserves marked to show the assembled Maori who had gathered to sign the Deed. The plan was possibly drawn by Park but is now thought to be lost. The signing was accomplished aboard the *Deborah* on 26 July 1844. There was one incident in Otakou concerning Park after the signing, recorded by William Wakefield. £300 was to be paid to Karetai, £300 also to Taiaroa, and £600 to 'people'. The principal, Chief Tuhawaiki, who had received £900, arbitrated on the money. Karetai protested he was £20 short. A mistake? When Karetai reached shore he recounted. After all he had his £300. The 'head man' was accused of purloining the money, and then replacing it. 'John Tuhawaiki reproached Karetai with having told us lies, upon which he [Karetai] scratched John's face, who beat him. Karetai's son going behind him flourished a tomahawk over Tuhawaiki's head which was wrested from him by Mr. Park'. Tuhawaiki said he would not forget the insult, but he was to drown in November 1844, leaving Taiaroa as ariki of the area.

Robert Park's son writes that his father was unable to come to terms with Mr Tuckett 'and so returned to Wellington', while Colonel Wakefield and Barnicoat went to Nelson to arrange for more surveyors and men to go to Otago to survey New Edinburgh, the site for which had been settled on at the head of the harbour with Port Chalmers as the port. Tuckett had a long wait in Port Chalmers in the brick and timber cottage he had put up earlier. Word came eventually that the Company had run out of money and the complement of surveyors and men who were set to come on the chartered *Carbon* from Nelson were all laid off. In December Tuckett returned north, leaving surveyor Davison alone at Port Chalmers to keep the place warm. It would be 14 months before he would see his colleagues again, and longer still before the Scottish immigrants left their homeland.

Park, back in Wellington, went on with his private practice. An advertisement on 2 November 1844 lauds the 'valuable property' of the 'Kai Whara Whara Estate' which was 'laid out judiciously in lots to suit purchasers by Robert Park Esq.' This estate had 'valuable water privileges'. The Kaiwharawhara had been settled by Scottish immigrants, not far along the waterfront from Thorndon Quay in the town. A road had been formed through to here in the 1840s but was scarcely more than a foot track until 1845 when the Army made it suitable for bullocks and horses – a bridle track ran over the hill from Kaiwharawhara to Tawa and on to Porirua.

In February 1845 Robert was writing to his sculptor brother Patric congratulating him on his marriage to Robina Carruthers of Inverness back home in Scotland. The letter with all its vagaries of grammar and spelling is quoted in full here, as it is the only known surviving letter of this period. It was not an official letter, so Park is free to express his unvarnished opinions and feelings on people and places.

Wellington 19th Feb. 1845

Dear Patric

I received your note of 24th Septr to days ago informing me of your intended marriage and since then have seen with pleasure in a Glasgow Herald that the affair has taken place I am of as few words as yourself and have therefore only to wish you long life and happiness and plenty of "bairns" give your wife an extra kiss on the reception of this note (You see I pay you back in your own coins for the same reason that I have little or nothing to write about) and tell her that I hope to have the pleasure of shaking her b the hand one of these days and presenting my children to their cousins in England. We are horribly dull here my Dear boy what with a mad Governor a bigoted Bishop and all the other etceteras of bad government We are at present a ruined Colony however we expect some amusement shortly from the freakes of our Governor as he has written for more troops to Sydney to compel a certain Ehone Heke to treat the British flag with a little more ceremony than he has hitherto done You will see by the NZJ better than I do describe it how this Mouri has insulted the British & Fitzroy so his Excellency finds at last that the natives are not the fine race he tried to make out and to force down the throats of those in the know them better than himself he now considers that nothing but sanguinary measures will keep them in order & so after having by his former folly tempted them on to insult him he now turns round and says he'll shoot them We expect that there may be a skirmish in the valley of the Hutt about 10 miles from Wellington but as it is a government matter (if it comes to fighting at all) between the soldiers sailors & natives we taking no part in the thing but it is of the utmost consequence that we should get possession of the Hutt as it is our most valuable district the natives are to go next month & some of them tell me they intend to go peaceably but that will depend upon the front shown by the govent Until the Mouri get a good dubbing and the pride is taken out of them we cannot expect to proceed or succeed in any one thing and it is only one good thrashing that is

required to tame them down to better behaviour My two brats are both
well & is Mary Ann who sends her complts to Mrs Patric Park & now
for lack of further matter & the ship leaves in two hours I must bid you
adieu and believe me your afft brother Bob I am writing to Catherine at
this time likewise.

The Kaiwharawhara subdivision was the reason for the Ngati Tama chief of that place, Taringa Kuri, to move to the Hutt at the invitation of the tribe who were the principal owners of the land in the valley, which Park speaks of as 'our most valuable district'. The land was not the Company's although the now deceased Governor Hobson had, in 1841, allowed a few settlers to occupy land providing no Maori cultivations, pā or burial places were disturbed. Tensions over the years inevitably mounted with more settlers eager to own land and farm there. As Park says, agreement had been reached that after the March harvest the tribes would leave peaceably and compensation be given which Commissioner Spain had determined should be awarded before any settlement could be finalised. By December 1844, though, it had become clear that more land was being cultivated by Maori and the tribe was still there. (In fact the Maori in the Hutt valley had been feeding Wellington.) Park echoes in his letter the feelings of the Wellington people. Despite the earlier efforts at arbitration, this would be set aside in the face of the rising anger of the would-be settlers, and troops would be brought in to enforce the Maori departure. Taringa Kuri protested – where would he go now? He'd left Kaiwharawhara because of European pressure – he would stay in the Hutt.

But now news came that Kororareka in the Bay of Islands had been sacked – the name 'Ehone Heke' and his 'insults to the British flag' were all the talk. The first priority now for the troops which Governor Fitzroy had called for was to put the northern rebellion down. Major Richmond in Wellington decided that the time had come to erect forts and places of safety for women and children in Wellington and the Hutt. One of these was at Kaiwharawhara, at the beginning of the road leading to the Hutt, and at the Hutt itself. The other was up the valley near the Town of Richmond shown

A Robert Park depiction of 'Maori dwellings and chapel and whaler's lookout ... near Kaiwharawhara' ca 1842.

Drawings and Prints Non A.T.L.-P-0004 A.T.L.

in Park's 1842 lithograph. Now he sketched Fort Richmond. Work had begun in April, and the whole was completed in July 1845. Authority was given in May to raise volunteer companies which, anticipating this development, had begun drilling in April. Robert Park was a lieutenant in the militia. More Maori came to the Hutt valley to cultivate and by August 1845 it was apparent that force would be used to evict them.

The troubles that came to the Hutt and to Porirua in early 1846, when Grey replaced Fitzroy as Governor, after all did not concern Park. He, Mary Anne, and his two 'brats', Mary Jane and Agnes, were by then in Port Chalmers, Otakou.

Stockade R. Hutt

The Fort Richmond Stockade on the Hutt River 1845. R.Park.

Couresy David Deans Estate.

CHAPTER 6

NEW EDINBURGH – DUNEDIN 1846-1847

As most readers will know, 'Dunedin' is the old name of Gaelic derivation for Edinburgh.

It was to lay out the town of Dunedin for the impending arrival of the Scottish settlers that an advertisement appeared in the *New Zealand Spectator* in Wellington for surveyors to tender for surveys of over 100,000 acres at 'prices per acre' for 10-acre and 50-acre sections at New Edinburgh.

Here was an opportunity for Robert Park. With the troubled state of affairs in Wellington, Mary Anne's nervous disposition, and with his love of all things Scottish, he may have thought of the possibility of staying permanently amongst his own folk, the anticipated Scottish immigrants. He was employed as assistant surveyor to Charles Kettle. With Kettle, Robert and his wife, Mary Anne, and the two girls Mary Jane (4) and Agnes (2½) and 'a girl' – a servant presumably – set sail on the *Mary Catherine* on 19 February 1846 for Otakou. Aboard, too, were 25 labourers at 14 shillings a day, some few with wives, and other surveyors who were to tender for the selected surveys by 30 March. Robert Park's diary recorded the arrival of the *Mary Catherine* at Otago Heads on 23 February. *Breeze continued; land in sight Kept on till 6 oc pm when we entered the harbour unfortunately the wind failing us we drifted on to the bank on the W spit where we suffered a severe thumping sent the women on shore to be out of the way. After laying out a hawser astern we got her off and anchored in the harbour vessil strained a little making some water.*

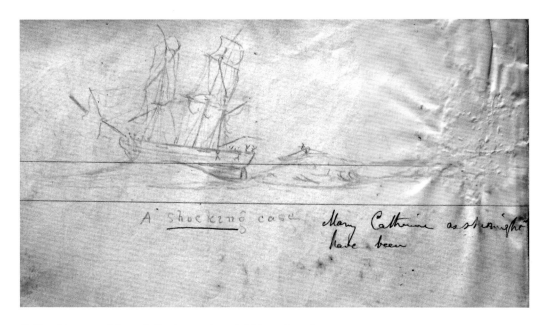

'A Shocking case. Mary Catherine as she might have been'.
R Park FB 8 LINZ Dunedin.

Kettle, in a report to Wakefield, makes light of the incident, although he comments that it would have been better to have accepted the services of the pilot who had come alongside when they were passing Taiaroa Head at the entrance. The pilot was very likely Maori. It was a Mr Driver however who, when the flood tide helped float them off the sandbank, took them safely to anchorage opposite the old native village of Koputai – to be renamed very soon Port Chalmers, and to be the port for New Edinburgh.

Surveyor Davison, his enforced isolation finally over, came aboard early the following morning and, wrote Kettle, 'returned again to Koputai … to receive the stores etc. which I had conveyed to that place in sealing boats' on the evening of the 23rd. There had been, since December 1844, a rough jetty built, and the stores were by evening all stowed in the Company's store. A few settlers had arrived from around New Zealand

Sawyers Bay. Almost part of Port Chalmers in the next bay to the south. Here a mill cut timber for early boat building at Port Chalmers.

Robert Park. Courtesy David Deans Estate.

Far Left: The Scotswoman, Mrs Anderson, of Port Chalmers?

Left: Surveyor colleagues.

R Park FB 8 LINZ Dunedin.

Port Chalmers, Otago. 1850. The New Zealand Company's store and the house where the Park and Kettle families lived is to the right of the road heading over to Sawyers Bay.

William Fox Pictorial Collections. Hocken Library. University of Otago.

anticipating settlement after the 1844 purchase. Still at Koputai was Alexander McKay who had come at the end of 1845, and with relatives, the Andersons, had patched up the old surveyor's huts for their families to live in. McKay was still there and would provide food at 'The Surveyors Arms'. Davison, while the sole surveyor at Koputai, had made 'an excellent survey of the coastline of the harbour'. He was to further this marine survey by 'laying down the sand flats with accuracy'. Kettle would then decide on the position of buoys. Otakou was a busy harbour where ships, mainly whalers and sealers, came for shelter and to 'wood and water'. At this time, March 1846, there were eight ships lying at anchor as well as the *Mary Catherine*.

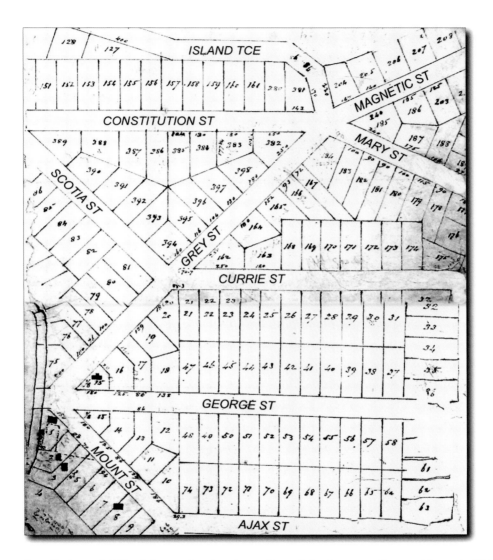

Port Chalmers field book layout showing the position of the Company Store and house in 1846 at the foot of George Street. (Printed street names have been added.)

R Park FB 8 LINZ Dunedin.

From Davison's surveys Kettle produced a plan in May 1846 showing the soundings in Port Chalmers harbour and an outline of the layout of the streets which he had 'ranged' by the end of February. Robert Park had set out immediately to lay off the streets of Port Chalmers with occasional help from Davison. Kettle thought that in about a month, that is the end of March, they'd be moving down to the site of Dunedin.

In the meantime, Kettle was off to the Molyneux and the other surveyors and the cadets – Drake, Scroggs, Charlton, Thomas, Wylie, Jollie, Abbott, Harrison, Watts and Tully – set about viewing the blocks they might survey. They had been all rather crammed for a time at Koputai, in the Company store, in tents and in the rough huts. The Parks too, although in the brick cottage which Tuckett had put up in 1844, had to share its three rooms with the Kettles. Each family had a room at either end with the central room a communal one.

Kettle was back in Koputai by 19 March when he had immediately set up the contracts with the surveyors. They set off to their chosen tracts on 9 April. On 15 April Robert Park began laying off sections at Dunedin, but the weather was bad and work slow. And came to a halt when the men struck for a pay rise for a couple

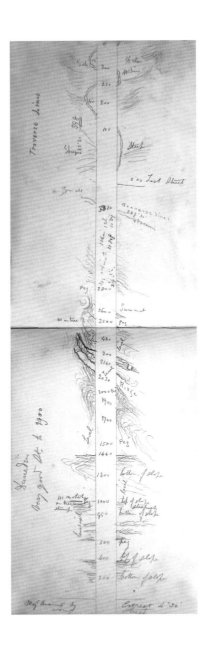

Survey of a trial road line from the waterfront in Dunedin on the line of the extension of the present Jetty Street - the first 19 chains noted as 'Very good St'. but the line later abandoned. The line of 'Last Street' is probably the present Arthur Street coming from the north near where the old York Street Cemetery would be.

R Park FB 8 LINZ Dunedin.

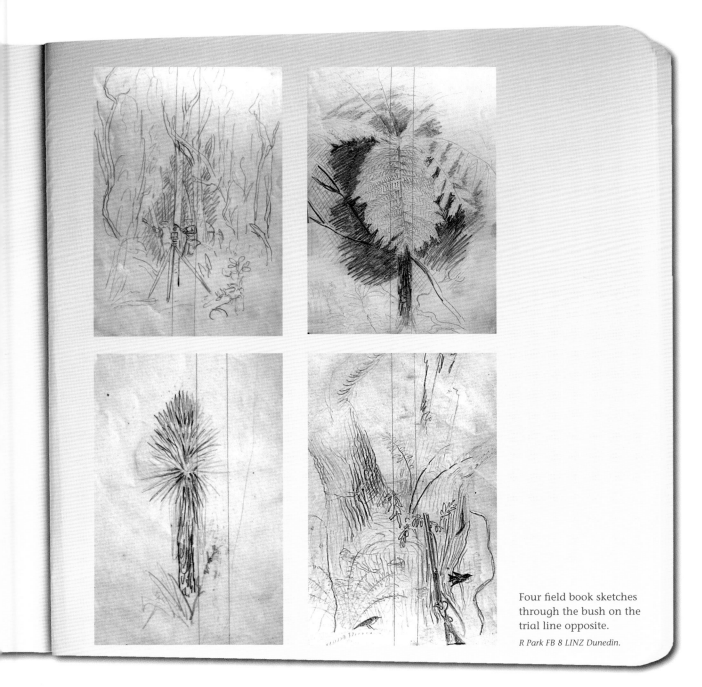

Four field book sketches through the bush on the trial line opposite.

R Park FB 8 LINZ Dunedin.

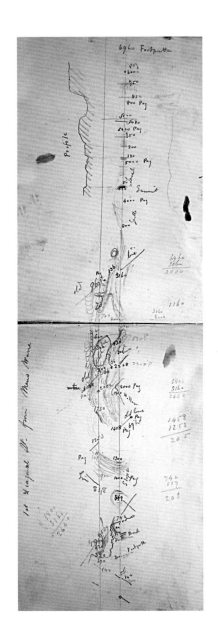

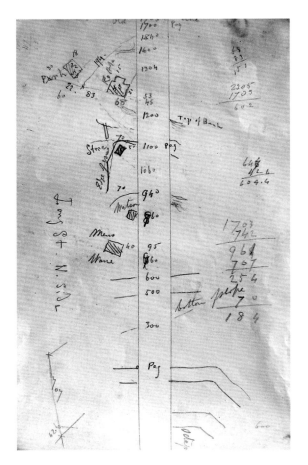

Above: Another road line survey from Princes Street towards the south west. '1st Diagonal St from Mens Warre' the present High Street? This line crossed the earlier abandoned line which is noted as 'old line' at 3160.

R Park FB 8 LINZ Dunedin.

Left: The line of Princes Street showing Kettle and Park's houses, the 'Men's Warre' and the Store.

R Park FB 8 LINZ Dunedin.

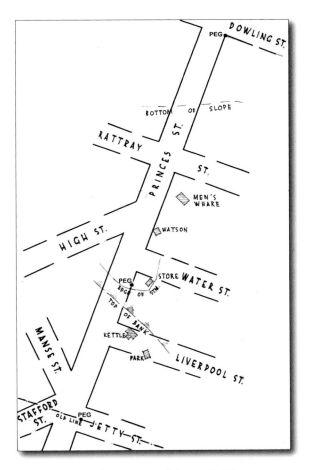

Sketch showing the position of the old buildings
relative to the roads today.

Frank Easdale.

of days at the end of May. Their pay was upped from 14 to 16 shillings a week plus rations. There was no more trouble. The bulk of the Dunedin town survey was completed by the end of 1846.

When the Parks moved to live at Dunedin is uncertain. Mary Anne had found herself pregnant once more (for the fifth time) and on 2 August a son was born, at Port Chalmers. The only record of the birth is in the baptismal register kept by a Methodist Minister, the Rev. Charles Creed, who would, from time to time, come over from his mission station to the north of Otakou at Waikouaiti to perform these offices of the church. Someone has added (in another hand) in the register the place of birth as 'Akaroa' which has given rise to a certainty by some that it was so. It is just wrong. A notice appeared in a Wellington paper on 22 August of Patric's birth at 'Otakou'. Patric

Park (named for his sculptor uncle) was baptised on 29 October 1846 when the Parks' residence is given as Dunedin, Otakou. Kettle is thought to have left Port Chalmers for Dunedin about November 1846. A lean-to wooden kitchen from the brick cottage at Port Chalmers was towed up harbour to serve again at the Dunedin site.

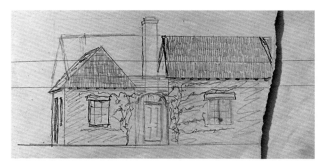

Did Robert Park think the family might settle in Dunedin? A plan in a field book and the sketch shown, would certainly indicate plans for a more comfortable and commodious home.

R Park FB 8 LINZ Dunedin.

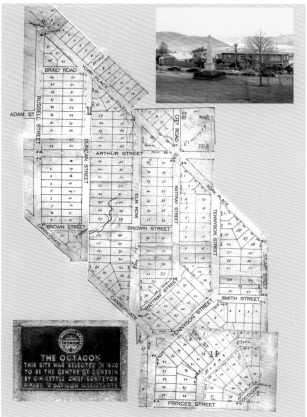

Compiled sheets from Park's fieldbooks show the layout as it was surveyed. Roads unnamed at the time (1846) have been added in print. The photo at the top shows the monument to those buried in the old York Street Cemetery, now a park reserve. Baby Patric Park would have been laid to rest here. Although there is no record of the very early burials, it would have been one of the first in the cemetery. The photo at the bottom is the plaque placed in the Octagon to commemorate the selection of the site of Dunedin by surveyors Kettle, Park and Davison.

Photos Frank Easdale.

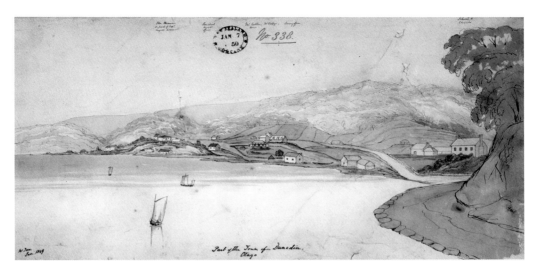

'Part of the town of Dunedin, Otago' by William Fox January 1849 drawn for the New Zealand Company. Park's old house and Kettle's are either side of what is now Liverpool St.

Drawings and Prints b-113-005 A.T.L.

Apart from the plans and sketches from Robert Park's field books, some memories of his daughter Agnes had been garnered over the years and were published by her son in the *Lyttelton Times* after her death in 1927. She recalls her Dunedin of 80 years before. Although she was only 2½ when they arrived at Port Chalmers, by the time they left Dunedin in June 1847 she was just on 4. Old enough to tell of the store with a 'bag of black sugar at the door, and two cottages'. The Park cottage possessed the only fence, and was close to the beach, where her father kept his boat, to reach which he wore long wading boots. While at Port Chalmers, she told her son, the family was joined by Martha Morgan a 23-year-old sister of Mary Anne, fresh from England. It was as well perhaps to have her sister with her when baby Patric died. This very early Dunedin death is not in any records, but the little fellow is at rest in the old York Street Cemetery. The son's account has the death as that of Agnes' 'older' brother, but is this later confusion that of Agnes or her son?

Agnes Park, at about three years, drawn by her father.

A page from a field book scribbled on by Agnes and 'autographed' for her by her father.

Could this woman with her face hidden by her bonnet be Mary Anne's sister Martha Morgan?

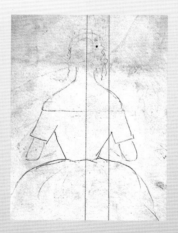

And is this perhaps a back view of Mary Anne with her side curls?

A back view of Robert Park in his long boots as his daughter Agnes later described?

R Park FB 8 LINZ Dunedin.

For the months up to June 1847, Park had gone on with further surveys, extending the town sections, and of the harbour. Then he received notice on 10 June that his services would be no longer required. Once more the New Zealand Company was in financial difficulties. The settlement of Dunedin by the Scots pioneers would not happen for a further nine months. They would be escorted up the harbour in March 1848 by the pilot Driver, so esteemed by Kettle, and the fine Maori crew from Taiaroa Head. Kettle was there to welcome them. His life thereafter would be centered on Dunedin. Robert Park's would not, and although he went on working until 13 June, when

Two views of Otakou (Otago) Harbour sketched by Robert Park. Scottish nostalgia is in the name 'Isle of May' which lies at the entrance to the Firth of Forth.

R Park FB 8 LINZ Dunedin.

he began selling off his things, on 12 July, after departure had been delayed by heavy gales, their ship sailed for Wellington. And he could not know as their ship sailed past Taiaroa Head to the open ocean that this place which he would not visit again would be important to two of his children yet to be born. The family arrived on 18 July at Wellington – a long trip – four days down, but six back.

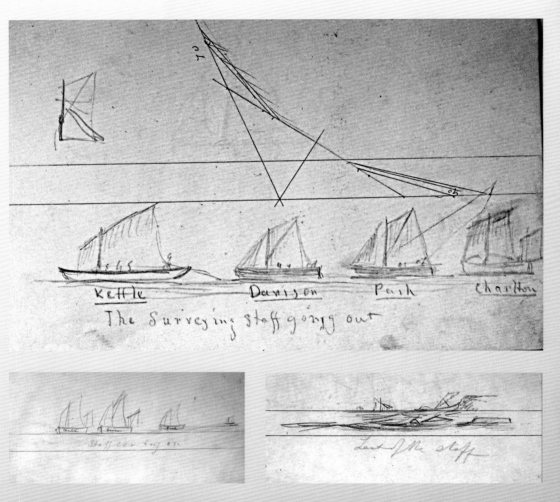

The sketches contain the following handwritten labels:

Kettle   **Davison**   **Park**   **Charlton**

The Surveying Staff going out

Staff coming in

Last of the staff

Trio of sketches offering a commentary on harbour surveying. 'The Surveying Staff going out', Kettle as leader towing a reluctant Davison, Park & Charlton. 'Staff coming in', Charlton in front with Kettle well to the rear. 'Last of the staff'. Disaster is always just around the corner!

R Park FB8 LINZ Dunedin.

A coat of arms for the Dunedin survey team. 'Never Say Die' – a motto for the
axe-wielding supports, guarding the useful bottles. And next to it an alternative
crest and motto for those who shared both work and jollity – 'For each his deserts!'
R Park FB 8 LINZ Dunedin.

Park, it appears, had enjoyed his time in the south (even if he did not care for Kettle who he was to later call, along with Stokes, a hypocrite and a liar!). It was in Dunedin that these surveyors acquired elevated nicknames – Charles Kettle was dubbed *'Lord Charles Kettle of Dunedin Hall'.* There were *General Thomas K. P. & Sir Robert Harrison of Archangel & Odessa, Sir Andrew Wylie of that ilk alias Oily Gammon, Col. Jollie, 'Admiral' Sir Francis Drake, Dr. Isaac Watts . . . Capt. Scroggs alias Count Scrogici, General Tully, Count Abbott . . . Sir William Davison of Humbug House . . . Baron Charlton of Otago & Koputai.* And inevitably Robert Park received the soubriquet of *Mungo Park of Holyrood.* What else? After all Mungo Park was held up as a hero to boys and men of that century. 'Holyrood' had no connection, but never mind, a castle of the royal Stuarts sounded suitably grand. Holyrood may have been dropped but it seems the nickname 'Mungo' may have been remembered for some time.

CHAPTER 7

WELLINGTON AGAIN
1848 – 1850

The Parks came back to a livelier Wellington in mid 1847 than the town they had left in February 1846.

In Otakou they had been removed from the troubles which had beset the settlers. The skirmishes in the Hutt and at Plimmerton were long finished but the troops brought in to quell the uprisings were still about, their coats adding splashes of colour to the streets. Now there were picnics, soireés and balls. The little Park sisters were too young to be a part of this, but their Aunt Martha at 23 wasn't and it was high time she married. The 65th Regiment, which had been building the road from Kaiwharawhara to Porirua Harbour (where they were stationed), was still about. Martha would after a time give her heart and hand to Joseph Osbertus Hamley of the 65th Regiment (Ordnance).

Christmas came and went, and on 1 January 1848 Mary Jane Park turned six. Just three weeks later her beloved mother Mary Anne died, giving birth to a stillborn son. They were buried just over the western fence of the Park Cottage property which bordered the Bolton Street Cemetery, where the other baby son, Robert Wakefield, had been laid to rest eight years before. A measure of Robert and his daughters' grief at their loss is inscribed on the tombstone.

A self portrait by Robert Park. And perhaps the ringletted young woman he painted dressed in the style of the 1840s might be Mary Anne? No portrait of Mary Anne has been found and her time in New Zealand was too early for photos.

Courtesy David Deans Estate.

> *Gone is that sunny smile that laughing eye*
> *Mute that sweet voice I lov'd so much to hear*
> *Forever still'd the mother's watchful sigh,*
> *Forever dried the wife's consoling tear.*

But perhaps never more poignantly did Robert's heartbreak show than in some verse in a field book. Only two short months after Mary Anne was buried he had to be a witness at a court case, concerning property of Scott's which had been deferred while he was in Otago. A poem, his own or borrowed, it doesn't matter, runs across a page of field notes, in thick soft pencil.

'View of Wellington from Major Baker's verandah, about 1848.' The pregnant Mary Anne Park could have sat here with her sister Emily Baker looking across the Wellington Harbour to Petone, the first New Zealand Company settlement. Mary Anne's little daughters Mary and Agnes at about 4 and 2 might have played in this garden with their small cousin Frederick Baker shown in the painting.

Water colour by Major Richard Baker. Drawings and Prints C-014-015 A.T.L.

And art thou dead? I dare not think
That thus the solemn truth can be
And broken is the only link
That chained youth's pleasant thoughts to me.
Alas! that thou coulds't know decay –
That sighing I should live to say
'The cold grave holdeth thee'

. . . . . .

Eye hath not seen it
Ear hath not heard
Dreams cannot picture sorrow & death
Time doth not breathe on its fadeless bloom,
Far beyond the clouds & beyond the tomb.

It was probably a quiet wedding for Martha when she was married to Joseph Hamley by the Rev. Cole in the Anglican church at Johnsonville on the Porirua Road, on 27 April 1848. After all, she was still in mourning for her sister.

The 65th Regiment's band was much in demand and in May the Hamleys were present at the celebrations for Queen Victoria's birthday, when the band played on the Thorndon Flat and a royal salute was fired from *H. M. S. Meander* in Lambton Harbour. Were the Park children taken to this to cheer them up?

But there is a much bigger question. When did Robert Park seek solace with Terenui of Te Atiawa? She was a relative of Wi Tako Ngatata of Kumutoto Pā, who had assumed the cloak of his father Ngatata-i-te-rangi and of the the Chief Wharepouri of Ngauranga. Wi Tako's house was built near the Kumutoto Pā site not too far from Park Cottage at the end of Kumutoto Street. Wi Tako was planning to go to live at Ngaraunga (where Wharepouri's memorial was) and cultivate his land at the Hutt

It is tempting to think that this sketch of a Maori girl with a babe in arms could be Terenui with the infant Anihaka.

R Park FB 72 LINZ Wellington.

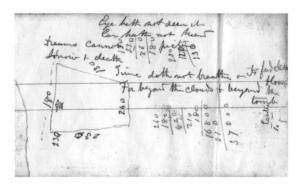

A page from a Park field book with his poetic lament for the loss of his beloved Mary Anne.

FB 60 LINZ Wellington.

Probably sketched from Ohau Point south west of Wellington looking up the coast to Mana and Kapiti Islands and the entry to Porirua Harbour.

R Park FB 43 LINZ Wellington.

where the Chief Te Puni held sway. Little is known of Terenui, apart from her highborn status, and of her relationship with Park. What is known is that she gave birth to a daughter in 1848-49, Anihaka. A grandson, Harry Park wrote that Park was married by Bishop Hadfield, but that the register in which this was recorded was burnt in a fire at Otaki some time later. The Reverend Octavius Hadfield as he was then, had been ill in Wellington for some years and was not practicing as a priest. It could be doubted too that he would, had he been able, conduct a secret ceremony with four other participants. I can find no evidence of a marriage or of a fire in which registers perished and I doubt if Robert Park and Terenui's union was blessed by the Church.

Terenui's daughter Anihaka was 40 (according to her marriage certificate) in December 1888. '40' is a good round number and it is quite probable that she didn't know her exact birth date. She could have been born in 1849. It is hardly to be believed that the intensely sorrowful Robert, writing his heartbroken verse in March 1848, would have had a liason with Terenui to produce a child in December 1848. And yet it may have been so. Grief may find solace in surprising ways.

One has to ask: even if they had been married following the birth of Anihaka, why there appears to be no knowledge of this in contemporary writings? There is not a whisper of this in Wellington. Park was such a public figure that anything more than a

Wreck of the *Tyne* 6 July 1845. On the back of this sketch there is a note (in Park's hand) 'The time this sketch is supposed to be taken is about ten o'clock on Sunday morning July 6th, it faithfully represents the situation of the vessel and the boat in which four hands were endeavouring to land at the moment of the swamping of the boat by a heavy sea'.

R Park Drawing and Prints B-089-006 A.T.L.

fleeting relationship would surely have not gone unnoticed. And what about his daughters. Where were they? (This will be discussed again in the last chapters.)

It is needful to go back to see what Robert was doing during 1848. He was in Wellington for that year. Some land purchase boundaries needed defining out towards Cape Terawhiti and during 1848 Samuel Scroggs (Count Scroggici from Otago) and Dighton, a Maori, set off with Park, camping their first night in a bay beyond where the *Tyne* had been wrecked off Sinclair Head in 1845. Park had sketched the wreck. The following day they reached Terawaite Jack's station and went down to see Maori at Waiariki Pā, and slept that night at the station. Then on to Oteranga Bay. From here they walked to the top of a high hill (Terawhiti) to view the features of the land. There are no more field book diary notes but almost certainly Park made his field book sketch of the coast not far from here, possibly from Ohau Point.

Calling tenders for Beach Road.

New Zealand Spectator.

A survey by Park was advertised at the end of July 1848 at Johnsonville on the Porirua Road (where Martha Morgan and Joseph Hamley had been wed). Robert Park was also calling tenders for a seven-foot-wide footpath to be made of 220 split totara posts, along the Beach Road (Thorndon Quay), and for brick drains on Lambton Quay. The sealed tenders were to be in by 5 August at Mr. Park 'The Surveyor of the Works office'. Was this work done only to be undone on 16 October 1848 when a severe earthquake jolted the town? The quake began at 1.30 a.m. with 'a sound like subterranean thunder, accompanied with a vibration of the ground for a few seconds, and then a quick heaving oscillation of the earth, which in a few seconds more died away with a quivering motion'. Further strong shocks followed on the 17th, 19th and 24th. Between these there were 'a great number of smaller shocks'. Robert Park was chosen by the inhabitants of Wellington to represent them on the three man Board set up to examine and assess the earthquake damage and its cost to repair, and to make recommendations as to future building practice.

Many people were alarmed at the continuing after-shocks and some took passage on the *Sobraon* which lay in the Wellington Harbour and was to call at Sydney on the passage home to England. Aboard were Robert Park's two little daughters Mary Jane and Agnes in the care of Mr and Mrs Fitzherbert. They were to go back to England to their Uncle Patric and his wife and their paternal grandmother in London, and according to Agnes (as later told to her eldest son), their father was to follow. Unbeknownst to Robert, Patric, in serious financial difficulties, had fled to Scotland in September and had settled with his wife and young daughter in York Place, Edinburgh. Their mother and their three sisters had remained in London.

However the *Sobraon* would not get to Britain, nor even Sydney. The barque 'was cast away by a drunken pilot' and wrecked at the Wellington Heads on 26 October. Two letters were published in the newspaper paying tribute to the coolness and self-possession of Captain Mills, whose one thought when the ship could not be saved was 'the preservation' of the women and children who made up most of the passengers. The energy and conduct of the chief mate and the crew was exemplary. Not a life was lost and the little girls were returned to their father. One letter was signed by a long list of passengers at the head of which were the Fitzherberts, then 'Robert Park, for Family'.

It may be doubted that Robert's intention in seeing his children embarked for Britain was to follow them later. Perhaps by now he had decided to stay with his new love, Terenui? He had been a signatory to a letter dated 16 September 1848 to

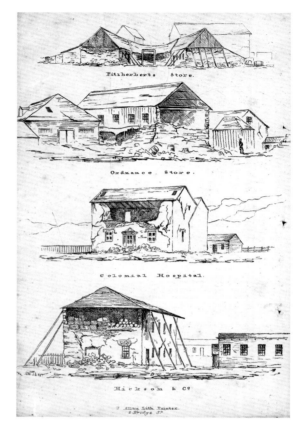

This lithograph shows damage sustained in the 1848 earthquake. The original sketches by Robert Park were held in the Public Record Office.

PUBL-0050-01 A.T.L.

the Principal Agent, Colonel William Wakefield, congratulating him on the recent amicable settlement between the Land Purchasers and the New Zealand Company, and to assure him of their certainty that the mutual confidence and good will that had united the 'first pioneers of British Colonisation' would see them go forward, founding

'Inside heads Wellington Harbour. Stormbird towing in.' The ship *Sobraon* with Park's two daughters was wrecked at the Wellington Heads in October 1848.

R Park. Courtesy David Deans Estate.

other settlements. This supportive and hopeful letter was signed by a number of old hands, including Robert's brother-in-law, Major Richard Baker, and, by proxy, his former companion in 1840 on the Wanganui foray, William Deans, who was now farming with his brother John Deans on the Canterbury Plains. Land was purchased from Maori in June 1848 (Kemp's Purchase) and the Christchurch survey begun in 1849. This letter was barely received by Wakefield when he died suddenly on 23 September. William Fox would become the Principal Agent of the Company and would greatly affect Robert's fortunes.

Maybe to cheer up Wellington people after the earthquake and Wakefield's death, the 65th Regiment's band were once more on Thorndon Flat giving a lively performance with excerpts from 'The Fair Maid of Perth', 'The Bohemian Girl', and works by Verdi and Donezetti, and ending with a valse, a polka and a gallop. A portion of the Regiment had been up to Wanganui where a large contingent was to be stationed in the future. At Wanganui, just five days before the wreck of the *Sobraon*, the *Harriet Leathart* had been driven on shore in a gale and wrecked on the Wanganui Bar. Martha's husband Joseph Hamley received a tribute for his part in the retrieval of goods from the abandoned ship. He was 'very active in the rescue'. The Highland Games were a highlight of December in Wellington when Governor George Grey and party were in town.

Military Encampment Wanganui ca 1848.

R Park. Drawings and Prints C-071-013 A.T.L.

Robert's future too was to be in Wanganui for a time. However, for the period from December 1848 through to mid 1849, Park went on with the local surveys. Who looked after the little girls? Perhaps someone lived in to care for them, or they went to their Aunt Baker (Jane Emily) for a time. In 1849 their father was appointed by William Fox as 'Principal Surveyor to the Wellington Settlement' at an annual salary of £400. This would be commensurate with what Park felt was his worth, and he needed the money. Fox informed the New Zealand Company that Park had 'a perfect knowledge of the surveys', together with 'a reputation which gives good weight to his authority'. It was something of a dilemma for Fox, when Park having accepted the position, Park's old boss

TO SURVEYORS,

TENDERS are required for the Survey of Two Blocks of Land about 6000 acres each, at Rangitikei and Turakina Rivers, and for a traverse of about 26 miles of the Waingaehu River.

Specifications and Maps to be seen at the New Zealand Company's Office. All tenders to be sent in on or before the 1st of October.

The lowest Tender will not necessarily be accepted, nor any Tender unless the terms are satisfactory.

ROBERT PARK,
Principal Surveyor,
New Zealand Company.
Wellington, 18th September, 1849.

Calling for tenders for survey of the Rangitikei Block.

New Zealand Spectator.

Mein Smith applied for the appointment. Captain Smith still smarted, no doubt, from being dismissed earlier in 1841 in a peremptory way. Park would diplomatically seek Mein Smith's assistance and expertise to lay out the Rangitikei Blocks and this action resulted in a comfortable partnership between the two men.

The purchase lay between the Rangitikei River and the Wanganui Block, bought in 1848 by Donald McLean an officer of the Crown, on behalf of the New Zealand Company but acting on Governor Grey's instructions. The Rangitikei land belonged to the Ngati Apa tribe, and on 15 May 1849 there was a large hui on the military parade ground in Wanganui. As a representative of the New Zealand Company, Robert Park was there, along with the 65th Regiment officers. On the 16th the land was weepingly farewelled, the deed signed. Payment was £2,500, £1,000 of which was given that day; the balance of £1,500 was to be paid in three more instalments over three years.

Donald McLean, as a land purchase negotiator with Maori, and Robert Park, the surveyor, would become close friends as well as colleagues. Robert, it was said, was McLean's 'favourite companion'. They were, while in Wanganui, staying in the 65th's quarters. Boundary surveys of the blocks within the Rangitikei land were undertaken from 25 July into August 1849. Park was already underway with the surveys when he received his formal appointment as Principal Surveyor to Wellington Province. He was, however, to continue to be based at Wanganui while working on the Rangitikei survey. Robert had left Wellington for a long stay at Wanganui in September informing the public that surveyor J. C. Drake would be attending to his business in his absence. McLean was also in Wanganui at Christmas 1849 and saw the New Year in in a traditional Scot's fashion, with a breakfast of 'old man's milk' – good Highland whisky.

'Maori Family outside a tent.' Near Wanganui, Attributed to R Park.
Drawings and Prints E-075-q-001 A.T.L.

In March 1850 McLean set out on a trip north to New Plymouth and on to Mokau and returned to Wanganui in April. But on 3 March 1850 Park is writing from Wanganui to 'Mac' saying he'd been expecting him daily for the last four months. He had heard though from the natives that he couldn't expect to see him until May. He'd been at Rangitikei for some two months laying off the blocks. A pole had been put up by the natives at Otaki at the mouth of the Porewa to show the whites the extent of the allowed purchase, and he was going back there in about a week. He is living in Gardiner's new house at Wanganui – 'very comfortable quarters' – and dining at the mess as usual. 'Life' he wrote 'goes on in much the same way as when you were here last only not quite so riotously'. At Easter 1850 Park is back at the Turakina ferry house reporting to McLean on surveys. He has 'sketched down the Rangitikei River from Parawenua' and surveyed the beach down to the ferry house. Tomorrow he is going on with the beach measurement north to the Whangaehu River. (These were the beaches he had walked in 1840

Parody on Byrons Solitude

To sit on chairs to muse o'er burning coal
To slowly trace the dinner on the board
Where things there be that own the Cook's control
Flesh, fish & Fowl that one can well afford
Nor grudge a glass of wine right good and old
Alone to eat and drink these things adored This is not
Luxury 'tis but to hold
Converse with Nature's charms & view her stores unrolled.

But midst a crowd, a set of hungry men
To see, to feel, to taste & to possess
One piece of beef, of mutton, sow or hen
With none to eat it, none to make it less
None who with hungry conciousness would eye,
If we were not, our tempting pleasing mess,
Would gobble, swallow, tho' to choking nigh
From such, to eat, sit alone, this, this is Luxury.

Parody by Robert Park
on Byron's 'Solitude'.

*Deans Family Papers,
Riccarton Bush Trust.*

to Wanganui and New Plymouth.) 'Oblige him by sending half a hundred weight of biscuit, some 20lbs of bacon, 8 pounds of sugar, 3lbs tobacco, two sailor's knives, some pipes matches and a small tinder box – (his) "worthies" have come badly provided.'

Park had evidently been back to Wellington, but in July 1850 was with McLean at the Rangitikei Heads along with Captain Daniell. Cottages are springing up in all directions here and there are fine fat oxen to be seen writes McLean to Susan Strang. Park teases him in his letter about his budding romance with Susan Strang. Everybody in Wellington, believes McLean to be engaged. Park had been asked 'by the Papa [solicitor Robert Strang] when you were coming down'. Park tells McLean 'you will have much to answer for when you reach that place'. He adds that Robert Hart the lawyer had made 'a desperate attack upon the young lady's affections' but hadn't succeeded.

Surveying at Turakina on the Rangitikei Block purchase.

R Park. Courtesy David Deans Estate.

Robert Hart, the successful lawyer and politician, would in a couple of years become Robert Park's brother-in-law and would eventually marry Donald McLean's sister Kate.

At Awahou (present day Foxton) the Governor [Grey] had bothered him 'about a Reserve commencing at & opposite that place & extending as far up as Parawhenua but of course I knew nothing of it'. He comments 'I do not altogether fancy his Excellency he is too vain & assuming however to please him as I wanted a canoe I staid with him on Sunday at Government ho'. Scottish humour? – Scott's boarding house or a tent? Oh, and could he please have some writing paper for one of his men who has been taken with a scribbling mania – 'he is likely in love … P.S. Some candles and salt'.

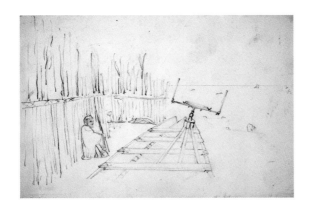

An alidade carried on the prow of a canoe from which Park would have taken observations.

R Park. Drawings and Prints A-215-012 A.T.L.

Both Park and McLean were in Wanganui in August 1850. McLean, reassuring his fiance Susan Strang of his safety, wrote that they'd been 'up the river in a fine large canoe with a crew of 16 men besides Mr Park and some chiefs. Two days brought us to Pukehika where there was a large feast with 1,500 natives assembled. Our share amounted to a ton of kumaras besides pigs, potatoes, birds preserved in their own fat'. A rough sketch was sent with McLean's letter to Susan (unfortunately lost?) showing 'Captain Campbell facing me wearing his broad Kilmarnock, and Mr. Park taking his observations in the last canoe as quietly as if he was sitting in a drawing room'.

The meeting of the waters. The Whangaehu which had its rise at Mt. Ruapehu's crater lake merges its cloudy and bitter waters with that of the dark Mangawhero. On the terrace above the latter is an extensive Maori kainga.

Whereabouts unknown.

83

On the Rangitikei River 1850.

R Park FB 67 LINZ Wellington.

Writing to Mac at Wanganui from Turakina again at the end of September, 1850, Park has only four sections to mark off. He had thought of surveying up the Turakina, but it was going to take too long so they (Pinnegar and Park) would instead walk up the river about 12–14 miles and strike a line from there which would about hit their line at Rangitikei. Captain Campbell, he has heard from Bell, is back in Wanganui. He sends his 'best respects' to him 'and old friends at the Mess'. When he began this letter he'd been having a midday meal with the 'Laird', the old Wanganui settler John Bell, but not much conversation as Park could not speak to him in Gaelic. This letter would be the last that Park as Principal Surveyor to the New Zealand Company would send to McLean. Once more the Company was in financial difficulties, this time so serious that it was finally wound up. Park, in under 12 months, found himself unemployed.

Into the picture, curiously, comes the Duke of Sutherland, for whom it may be remembered brother Patric had earlier done a sculpture back in Scotland. In November 1850 Earl Grey, the Colonial Secretary, has had a letter from the Duke 'expressing a great interest in Mr. R. Park'. Earl Grey then writes to Governor Grey saying he has informed His Grace that due to the New Zealand Company ceasing operations, it would give him great satisfaction if Park could be employed in 'public service'. The Duke of Sutherland (a Scot too) had been a sponsor of Park when he had applied to join the Company and had in fact acquired a section in the first ballot of land in Wellington, probably chosen by Park proxy. Earl Grey ended his request saying he should be 'very glad if it wd be in your power to meet the Duke's wishes on this subject'. The Executive Council of New Munster Province obliged the Colonial Secretary and Park had a job again in January 1851. Park was employed to survey the Ahuriri (Hawkes Bay) district, the purchase of which was being managed by Donald McLean. There is little doubt that Park's employment was managed too by McLean. After all they were both Scots, even if one was a Glaswegian, the other a Highlander. McLean had selected Park, as he reported, because he was 'good with the natives, practical, correct and expeditious'. Nevertheless, Park took a considerable drop in his salary going from £400 to £300, and that too was to be inclusive of all forage and travelling allowances. Pelichet would also be employed at a mere £150. Park was to employ native assistance 'as is absolutely necessary'. The government brig when it returned from Lyttelton would take the surveyors up to Ahuriri (to become the city of Napier). But this appointment came in January 1851. What was Robert Park doing up until the end of 1850? Certainly in September he is surveying at Rangitikei. In October 1850 McLean and Park had another meeting with Ngati Apa at Parewanui, Rangitikei. From here they went on to McDonnell's Accommodation House at Turakina where McLean slept. McDonnell 'kept some real Highland whisky which he, through his usual excess of hospitality, compelled me to drink, rather too freely, no doubt' wrote McLean. All Scots present had, he said, a 'wee bit talk about the McLeans, that rather rose my temper as high as the spirits we were drinking'. Park was staying at Tylee's, and the following day solicited McLean 'to join in a pledge between ourselves that we should abandon drinking of spirits, as the effect of last night's ride, and a few glasses of gin caused some excitement that annoyed him'. McLean agreed willingly to give up spirituous liquors – Park's pledge was to give up wine and beer as well. Would they have stuck to it?

Later in the month they were back in Wellington. What was Park doing during the next two months? Although he was at a ball at the Mess House in Wellington at the end of November, Donald McLean is away, and Park, who attended the ball, told Susan Strang that he was very sorry for her sake that Donald was not there. There were, of course, his daughters to see to who were happy no doubt to have their Papa home. Whether he had ever seen Terenui again and whether he knew that she had died giv-

A romantic view possibly painted by Robert Park about 1848-49.

Courtesy David Deans Estate.

ing birth to a son Huta in December 1850, is obscured in later stories. It is said by Huta's eldest son Harry that she died at Pipitea Pā, and was taken away by Huta's future father-in-law on a dray, against other relatives' wishes, to the Maori cemetery at Petone and buried there. Although Harry is much astray on the history of his Pakeha forefathers, here he would be more reliable. With the sad death of Terenui went first-hand knowledge of her relationship with Robert Park. He would never see his Maori/Pakeha children, Anihaka and Huta, as they grew and they did not learn of their

Pakeha heritage from British relatives. What they were told came from their Maori relations, which is why so many myths of their Pakeha origins were spawned when one particular descendant of Robert and Terenui told his version of events down the years.

Marion Hart, Robert Park's future wife, now comes on to the scene. George Hart (solicitor Robert Hart's brother) had gone back to England and returned with his widowed mother and his sister in November 1850. On 14 January 1851 Susan Strang wrote to Donald McLean that she had been seeing a good deal of Miss Hart. 'She is exceedingly pleasant in her manner and I think she is very clever and well educated.'

Susan Strang, her mother and father, Marion Hart, Miss Kelly and Miss Reddish had enjoyed an expedition to Pahatanui via Porirua, but at 'Boltons' they were 'teased' at night by mosquitoes. Susan and Marion tried lying on the floor wrapped in blankets and veils, no use, then on the beds. Others sat up and eventually went out to the cart. Then it rained. Nobody got much sleep.

In the same letter Susan told Donald that Mr. Park had been very ill. 'He had a severe fit of paralysis about three weeks ago, but I am happy to say he is very much better'. He was sufficiently recovered at least to take ship to Ahuriri (Napier) on 14 January 1851.

CHAPTER 8

EASTWARDS TO HAWKES BAY 1851

'Ahuriri 12th. Feby 51
Dear Mac,
Here I am at this blessed place which I think is about the last God made as it is in a most unfinished state.'

Park's 1851 Ahuriri (Napier) Harbour Survey. The Pā on Te Pakaki Island shows a stockade and a few whare. A few buildings on the Eastern Spit are just discernible. On the Western Spit is McKain's hotel as will be seen on Commander Drury's chart. From Villers and McKain in 1851, Donald McLean bought a house and outbuilding for £26 to house the survey party. The view is drawn from Battery Point. The land in the distance is possibly Tangoio Bluff.

Deans Family Papers, Riccarton Bush Trust.

Not an unusual reaction of newcomers finding themselves, as did Park, on the waterless shingle spit at the entrance to the harbour at what would become the town of Napier. Park had 'accepted with a grumble' the £300 a year offered by the Government, as he was told it would lead to something better.

He was annoyed, too, that Governor Grey had appointed Pelichet as his assistant as he would have preferred Pinnegar. Really, he railed to McLean, the management at 'the Government Offices is very bad and sadly wants remodelling' – it was four days before he could get them to buy instruments from the defunct New Zealand Company. 'I had to run from the Col. Secretary to Governor and back again until I was almost mad with vexation.' He has brought a lot of letters for McLean with him as he was hoping to see him.

But McLean was still away to the north of Ahuriri, to Mohaka and Wairoa going as far as Turanganui (Gisborne). McLean had, since arriving in Hawkes Bay, been active in holding meetings with the influential chiefs of the district, in particular Hapuku, Moananui and Tareha. He had written to Hapuku from Wanganui as far back as March 1850 of his proposed visit, so the tribes were well prepared and most were eager to negotiate the sale of land. McLean travelled to Hawkes Bay from Wellington through the Manawatu Gorge. Accompanying him were three chiefs of Rangitikei, who had land interests on the Wairarapa side of the Gorge. One of these was Kingi Hori te Tanea (King George).

WRIGGLESWORTH & BINNS   PHOTOGRAPHERS
WELLINGTON, N. Z.

Donald McLean.
Courtesy Heather Murchison.

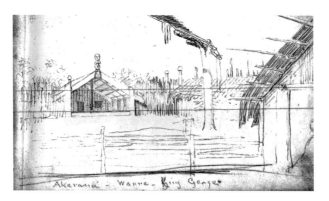

King George's whare Akerana. Kingi Hori te Tanea accompanied Donald McLean from Turakina to Hawkes Bay where this chief had land interests.

R Park FB 72 LINZ Wellington.

All were to be essentially helpful in encouraging Ngati Kahungunu tribes in welcoming the Crown representative.

When Park arrived at Ahuriri in early 1851, McLean had already been at Mohaka talking with the chief Paora (Paul) who had received them 'very kindly'. Robert Park would have much interest later in the Mohaka Block. Now he waited for McLean who returned to Ahuriri on 8 March. It may have been during this interval that Park fixed boundaries on the harbour shores. McLean also found Ahuriri 'an exceedingly dull place', and Susan writes him that she is 'glad Mr. Park is going to be with you for I am sure you must feel lonely sometimes when you have no one but natives to speak to'.

A week after McLean's return, he and Park were setting off south from Ahuriri across the swampy plain, and following one night's stop, having a lengthy korero with Tareha about the purchase of the 'Ahuriri Island', that is Matarahou, (later Scinde Island, now Bluff and Hospital Hills) considered essential to be part of the Ahuriri Block purchase as it commanded the harbour and its approaches. Maori were anxious to have substantial reserves here, for fishing and canoes.

The following day the party rode on to Omaranui, on the Tutaekuri River, where McLean and Park parted company, Park to traverse the boundaries of the proposed Ahuriri Block purchase. Park returned to Ahuriri in early April. He had been up the back of the block in the Kaweka Range which here divided Hawkes Bay from the Lake Taupo basin, where the Tuwharetoa tribe, with principal chief Te Heuheu, held sway. Te Heuheu was disputing the boundary at this time. His interests were to be met later.

Ruapehu. Tongariro steaming. From 'Kaweka 2 or 3000 feet above the sea'.
R Park 1969.122.11 Canterbury Museum.

On 14 April McLean is expecting Park's return to Ahuriri with about 100 or 200 natives. He and Park were both going 'to ride off into the interior after dinner'.

This was to meet with Hapuku and his people to discuss the price for Hapuku's Block (Waipukurau). Survey Assistant Pelichet with Captain Thomas had done the boundary work here walking it with the chiefs who pointed out the features such as rivers, hills, trees, rocks to figure in describing the block. Park rode out with Pelichet and Thomas, to be shown the Ruataniwha Plains. Noted McLean: 'Mr Park is highly delighted with the appearance of the country'. On 17 and 18 April the meeting took place with speeches and songs about giving up Maori claims to the land. It was left that

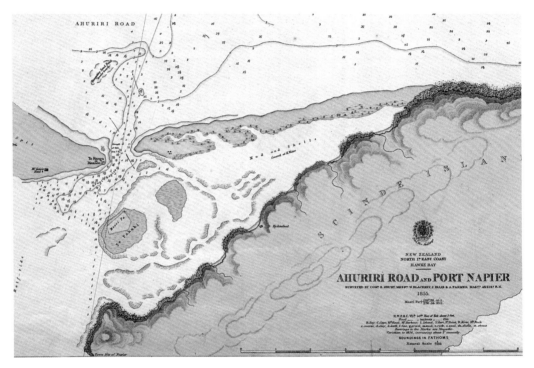

Ahuriri Road and Port Napier. Part of the chart of a marine survey by Commander B. Drury 1855.
Map Coll 832.3 aj4/1855 A.T.L.

Governor Grey's decision on the amount to be paid for the land would be accepted. Park and Captain Thomas again went out to the Waipukurau and the Ruataniwha so that a report of the land's 'capability' might be given to the Governor.

McLean was on the move again too, but on 25 April he was back and found the three surveyors and all their men quite snug at 'Survey Hall, Ahuriri'. This was a house built for them on the Western Spit. Snug they might have been but they wrote formally to McLean at the end of April, 'Sir – We have as you are well aware greatly facilitated the surveys by using our own horses, for which we are not allowed any forage money and we have the authority of Captain Thomas, late Chief Surveyor to the Canterbury Settlement for saying that one principal cause of the dispatch and cheapness with which his surveys there were executed was from his furnishing his Surveyors with horses'. They begged him to lay the matter before His Excellency Governor Grey, when back in Wellington. In Wellington Marion Hart, along with Miss Dorset and Susan Strang, had been a bridesmaid for their friend Ellen Reddish. The women's friendship was becoming a close one.

While McLean was in Wellington from May to October 1851, the boundaries of the Mohaka Block must have been fixed and it was probably during this time that many of Park's remarkable likenesses of named Mohaka people were sketched.

Robert Park is delighted at his friend Donald McLean's marriage to Susan Strang in Wellington in September 1851.

MS 0032-0491 McLean Papers. A.T.L.

Robert Park had put in his report to the Chief Commissioner on the Waipukurau, Ahuriri and the Mohaka Blocks, written in June 1851. He assesses the 'capability' of each block for farming, access, roading, and waterways. Waipukurau (Hapuku's Block), the largest area, had rich grassland and embraced a small portion of the Ruataniwha plain (some forty miles by ten). A plain which for 'beauty of position, fertility of soil, mildness of climate and abundance of wood and water stands unrivalled in New Zealand'. The main road from Port Nicholson to Hawkes Bay would pass through this block. The Ahuriri Block's value 'lay in the harbour consisting of a large sheet of water or lagoon, about five miles long by two miles wide, indented on the Western shore by beautiful little bays fit for residence and on the coast defended from the sea by a shingly spit'. The lagoon is nowhere more than nine feet in depth. On the North spit there is room for a small town and reclamation of 18 acres would extend the area for a 'lower town' and the island for the 'higher' with a channel widened and deepened. The lagoons to the south might by drained by canals. This is much as it fell out, apart from the canals, but then was so radically changed with the devastating earthquake in 1931.

The Mohaka Block Park said was 'a very pretty little purchase' with a fine river and a whaling station at its mouth. It would make three or four good runs, but the road 'as it at present runs, is execrable'. Another could be made inland. He sends two sketch maps, a general one overall, and one of the harbour entrance. The climate, he informed the Government, was 'magnificent, nothing can be finer'. It rains at night mainly and he had only lost three days in three months to wet weather.

On 6 September he wrote to McLean that he'd had two notes from him by the *Rose*, the schooner that ran regularly between Ahuriri and Wellington. Park has to congratulate him on his marriage – 'please give my best wishes to Mrs McLean'.

McLean wasn't wed until 28 September when he married Susan Strang, only daughter of Robert Strang, the Registrar General, in the Scotch Kirk in Wellington. Park would have calculated when the letter would arrive. He goes on to say that the drawing paper has come and he will be sending a large plan of the three blocks. A note adds that the maps are almost too large and the paper too thick to make a good job by folding them. Better get them mounted on cloth. He reckons he's been 'very economical for men' as he explains the bill he is sending. He doesn't expect to see McLean until well on into October, but he is so delighted with the idea of McLean as a married man that he ends his letter – 'With compts to Mrs McLean (I like) writing it over again just to remind you that you are no longer a batchelor [sic]'. Did he know that his ten-year-old daughter Mary Jane was at the wedding? – as was Susan's now dear friend Marion Hart.

McLean had set off on 30 September only two days after his marriage to return to Hawkes Bay with gold sovereigns in his baggage to pay the first instalments to the Maori owners of the proposed purchases. He came to Waipukurau where he met up with Park on 27 October. With McLean was Wi Tako Ngatata (the Wellington, Te Atiawa chief) who had always been such a staunch supporter of the New Zealand Company officials, and also of Government. (And now related to Robert Park through Terenui and their two children, Anihaka and Huta. Wi Tako was said by one descendant to have 'given' Terenui to Robert Park.)

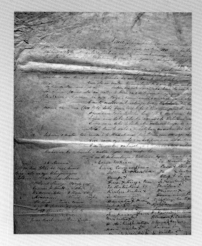
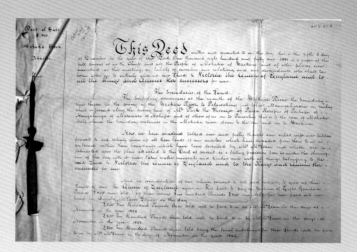

The Deed of Sale, 5 December 1851. Robert Park is named here as the surveyor of the Mohaka Block. Written in both Maori and English the Deed had near 300 signatures appended. Some were children who were to be witnesses of the future to their parents having signed. This Deed was witnessed, among others, by Wi Tako Ngatata, the Wellington Chief who had been an advocate of the sale of Ngati Kahungunu lands through Donald McLean, to the Crown.

ABWN 8012 W5279/210, HWB40 Archives New Zealand/Te Rua Mahara o te Kawatanga, Wellington Office.

Far Left: The Conveyance Document.

Left: The attached delineation by Surveyor Robert Park of the Mohaka Block.

All the sketches on the following 'album' pages are from the Robert Park sketch book.

GNZMS-349 Special Collections Auckland City Libraries.

Titled 'A few Maori heads roughly taken off by R. Park', this sketch book came back to the Auckland Public Library from the Sir George Grey Collection in Capetown South Africa in 1999. A wonderful source of named Ngati Kahungunu people the book is full of delightful pencil sketches, a number of which are reproduced here. A few have been identified as signatories to the Mohaka Deed. Some signatories to the Mohaka Deed identified as sketched by Park are on this page:

Far left: Kukuku.

(p.84)

Left: 'Moananui's wife. Moananui was the paramount Ahuriri Chief.

(p.83)

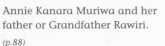

Annie Kanara Muriwa and her father or Grandfather Rawiri.

(p.88)

Paora te Rerepu, the young Principal Chief of Mohaka, with wife Lydia and baby Paul.

(p.103)

Manihera and Annetta, Manihera's wife with one of Hapuku's children Paora Rerepu again.
(p.80)

E Ware and [Poito?], two more wives with another sister of Hapuku and a Mohaka chief [Poito?].
(p.89)

Noa Noa, and his wife Emma Pirangi who signed the deed.
(p.102 and p.101)

'Something like Hapuku'.
(p.87)

Might this be Hapuku's sister Hine Paketia, known as the Queen of Ahuriri?
(p.76)

[Na Huka] One of Hapuku's 13 wives.
(p.78)

Te Kaka Iraia Kahitia.
(p.79)

Paia te Tera and his wife [Marahau?] with Magaretta Wharekura.

(p.90)

Maria Kokokakahu and her husband Hori [Mania?] Te Rangitira – Wai [Pakuroa?].

(p.106)

Pari Pari wife of [Hanga Munga] and two of her daughters.

(p.100 and 99)

Whakarongo

Hapuka deciding upon the leter for the land

Hapuku deciding on a price for the land. 'The Hearing.'

(p.108)

On 3 November the Deed was drawn up with Wi Tako making a list of the hapu (sub tribes) on 'clean sheets of paper'. Hapuku was evidently pleased that Governor Grey had increased payment from the earlier offer of £3,000 to £4,800 and after the signing of the deed on 4 November by Hinepaketia (Te Hapuku's sister the 'Queen of Ahuriri'), Hori Nia Nia, Karanine Te Nahu, Paora Te Ropitia, Tuhua and many others, and witnessed by surveyors Park, de Pelichet and Thomas, Wiremu Tako, settlers Collins, Tiller and Abbot, and the clerk Williamson, he wrote to Grey that now the Governor had the land would he send him settlers 'respectable European gentlemen'. 'I am annoyed' he continued 'with the low Europeans of this place … let it be a large, large, very large town for me.' Waipukurau was to stay a small country town. Ahuriri Port, to be named Napier in a few years, would be another story.

McLean and company were back at Ahuriri on 7 November. Some of the natives were starting to gather at Ongaonga Bay opposite the Eastern Spit. On Matarahou Island a house had been built by Maori 'for the Government'. Neat and commodious, it was the scene for the signing of the deed of purchase of the Ahuriri Block. Here McLean, and surveyors Park, de Pelichet and Thomas, with settler witnesses Curling and Abbott, sat on the native mats which covered over fine clean fern. There had been some difficulty in settling reserves on Matarahou Island, but now, with Park, McLean and chief Tareha having fixed the boundaries on 13 November the people on the 17th November assented to all the conditions. (This deed's provisions would, in the future, be questioned.) It is interesting that some children signed these deeds 'that they might be witnesses to future generations'.

Now there was just Mohaka and that was comparatively simple. On 5 December the deed was signed. The Mohaka people were 'acting well and as fine a set … as there is to be on the coast; they are hospitable and kind to travellers and deserve encouragement.'

There had been hanging fire the purchase of an additional block at Porangahau, adjacent to the Waipukurau purchase. On 17 December McLean, Park, Wi Tako, Hapuku, the 'Queen' and Hori Nia Nia Puhara went to view the 'good and handsome' block.

By 23 December McLean was back in Wellington, but when Park returned there is not known. However, at the end of December he was laying out the town at 'Ahuriri Harbour'. This is where Park, in his June report, had suggested a small town. McLean by this time had had a letter from the Colonial Office applauding him for the desire he had expressed to meet Earl Grey's wishes, by continuing to make use of Park's 'services'. Park's further appointment was under the Native Land Purchase Ordinance, from 1 January 1852 – McLean's Department. An amusing footnote – when after the Mohaka Deed had been signed, and he was about to leave Hawkes Bay, the canny McLean had 'disposed of several things, clothing etc. to Park and others', because, as he explained to his new wife, she wouldn't like him to wear such things and the cash would be acceptable to both of them!

When Park came back from Hawkes Bay to Wellington it was to find two miserable children, thin and bruised, if Agnes' memories are to be believed. Her son, writing of memories recounted to him, tells of the sisters' experiences at a school (unspecified) in Wellington, where they were 'tortured and starved', treatment which 'rivalled those of the wretched pupils at Dotheboys Hall', in Dickens' *Oliver Twist*. The son seems somewhat given to dramatic phrases. This schooling is said to have taken place over two years, while their father was engaged in the survey through the Seventy-Mile Bush to Hawkes Bay. Hawkes Bay is right, the other nonsense. And it wasn't two years, perhaps less than one, though to little people it may have seemed so. When Robert learned of his children's unhappiness, they were taken away from the female Squeers and sent as day scholars to a school at Thorndon Flat kept by a Miss Burbage (Burbridge?).

It is hard to understand why it was not known by Park that the children were suffering. After all, their late mother, Mary Anne, had her sister Jane Emily Baker living in Wellington. And wouldn't the girls have had holidays with their aunt? This is puzzling. They still had contact with her into adulthood so it doesn't seem likely that there'd been a falling out. It was time, perhaps, for Robert Park to seek a helpmeet again.

Marion Hart had been busy in company with her dear friend Susan McLean who was calling on people as a married woman. Robert had evidently begun courting Marion Hart in late 1851 and in an undated letter Susan writes of Miss Hart coming to take away some sewing she is doing for Susan. 'They all laugh at me for fretting about you being away but if Mr. Park is as affectionate a husband as my Donald, Miss Hart will miss him quite as much as I do you.' At Susan's on a Saturday when Marion 'went to put on her bonnet to go away she sat for I am sure an hour talking of her intended in my room. She seems very fond of him', although their acquaintance has been short. But what was 'the unfortunate business' in May 1852? It seems as though it may have been a moolight walk Marion took with Robert. In another letter Susan has written 'Moonlight walks are dangerous and I would advise young ladies to beware of them. I think our friend Miss Hart has found that out'. Ever since that night, Marion's mother has been against the marriage though quite agreeable to it at first. Marion tells Susan that she doesn't know what the cause of the change is, but her mother says she and Robert Park must now meet only as friends. 'She says that she is blamed for having taken that walk,' writes Susan 'which is a great shame as they only did what any other lovers would have done. It is that stupid Robert Hart who is to blame for the whole [and] has persuaded Mrs Hart to fret. It is very cruel to use his poor sister in this way.' She has asked Marion to come and stay for a few days but Marion declines not wishing to displease her mother.

Continues Susan to Donald: 'I feel very much for her I wish it could be settled but she seems to think there is no chance of it. It is very vexing that it is talked of so much. Everyone seems to believe that they are to be married soon … If you hear of it spoken of by any one do not say pet that there is any truth in it. Remember love that Miss Hart told all this in confidence so you must say nothing to Mr. Park about it.' And a day or two later, Susan writes that she hasn't seen Marion since Donald left for Rangitikei but remembers that when Robert last came in to say goodbye, the instant she had seen him Marion's face had become scarlet.

A few days later on 18 May, Donald writes to Susan from Rangitikei: 'Park is sleeping near me as I am writing away. He sends his compliments but I imagine although he does not confess it that he would like to send more than his compliments through you to Miss Hart'. He adds his kind regards for Marion, and says Susan may add as much more as she likes for Park. 'Did she shed a tear like my lassie when he turned up the

Kaiwarra glens.' A couple of days later she was able to give Marion the message that 'her dearly beloved was quite well' and arranged to spend a day with her.

'The marriage' she writes, 'is talked of so much here as being quite settled ... Every one I see speaks of it. It is a great shame that people will interfere and talk about what doesn't concern them.' She had suffered this herself before her own marriage to Donald. Susan finds later that Mrs Hart has had no change in her feelings and Marion 'had passed a most disagreeable week. They seem so displeased with her. She does not intend to say any more on the subject till Mr. Park's return. She will then ask for a decided answer but she has no hopes of it being a favourable one. I am sure it is all Robert's doing [as his brother] George is not against it. If Robert had any sense' laments Susan, 'he would not oppose it after having been the reason of his poor sister being talked of over the whole place.' Robert Hart's objection to the marriage may not have been based only on an unchaperoned moonlight walk as Susan believes. Could he have been aware of Robert Park's previous liason with Terenui? George Hart was away in England at that time 1848 and 1850, and quite certainly the ladies had not been told. Nor it seems did Park's friend Donald McLean know of the 'secret'. On 24 May Donald writes again from Rangitikei. He and Robert Park are going up country. He tells her that he feels 'much for Miss Hart and also for Park in this unfortunate affair'.

Things were looking up for Marion and Robert by July, though it is doubtful whether the Mamma or Marion's brother had yet relented. So eager is Susan to see her friend and Robert united that she arranges for them to meet alone. She and Miss Kelly have gone up to the Hart's home in Hobson Street and here found Marion was just on her way to see her. It was arranged that after Marion had been to the dressmakers in Willis Street she would then walk back over The Terrace where Susan lived. Robert, Susan knew, was coming to her home. When Susan and Miss Kelly got to the top of Willis Street they spotted Park going to Susan's house, so Susan said loudly to Miss Kelly so Park should hear, that 'she thought Miss Hart would get up easily on The Terrace as the roads were in such a state. Mr Park knew that I intended this for him as he looked up at me and laughed.' After a drink with these ladies he 'ran off as hard as he could down

Willis Street. I could not help laughing. It reminded me of our plans before marriage. How often we used to meet at Mrs Kirtons.'

Although Susan wanted Robert and Marion married, she did not approve of Park's forthright comments on 'poor Miss Kelly's religion', (that is Catholicism). She didn't think Park was much for religion, and she didn't care for him calling Paul the Apostle a humbug. She was sure his intended would not like to hear the way he had talked that night.

The last note we have from Susan McLean is in July 1852 when Park goes to Wanganui and Susan is going to see Marion to console her. 'I wonder if she feels the separation from her dearly beloved as much as I used to do'. Marion and Robert would not have to wait much longer for Robert Hart and his mother to relent for they were wed at last in September 1852. And it is possible, if speculation as to Robert Hart's objection is correct, that McLean was made privy to the 'secret' and was perhaps instrumental in persuading Marion's brother to forgive.

One of the Maori descendants writes that Robert Park married his 'housekeeper' a Miss or Mrs Hart. Certainly he married Marion Hart in 1852, but housekeeper? And his two other children, Anihaka and Huta? They had been taken by Maori relatives and now would be three years and one year, barely beginning to learn of their Pakeha heritage from their elders.

CHAPTER 9

WELLINGTON, WANGANUI, HAWKES BAY 1852 – 1854

On 24 October 1852 Robert Park wrote to Donald McLean from Wanganui: 'We arrived here safely on Tuesday afternoon the 19th after a pleasant journey and no accidents – I tried to get lodgings at Mrs Garners but she was very lofty & could not take us in; luckily I have no doubt it will turn out.

We are now in Jones house at the corner … & have been busy getting things in ship-shape order; borrowing here and buying there. On the whole I daresay we will manage to get on pretty well although we do sleep on straw beds & are not overburdened with furniture.'

Robert Park and Marion Hart had been married at Marion's bachelor brother Robert Hart's house in Hobson Street in Wellington on 23 September 1852 by the Rev. William. Kirton of the Scotch Church, the same reverend who had married the

Robert Hart's home in Hobson Street. Wellington. Where Robert Park and Robert Hart's sister Marion were married in September 1852.

R Park Courtesy Heather Murchison.

McLeans. Robert was now 40, his new wife 29. Now Marion, his wife of just a few weeks and the two daughters, Mary Jane and Agnes, from his first family were settling in at Wanganui. Agnes, the younger, was just nine, and was later to relate to her eldest son the adventure of the journey up. They travelled light, by dog-cart she said, the heavy luggage being sent by sea. She mentions one stop at Otaki, but there were several as Marion told Susan McLean in a letter of 1 November. They were following the route that Park had traversed in 1840. Not a lot had changed with much travel along the beaches, though there were now ferries at the major river crossings, and accommodation houses there. The first stop after Wellington was usually Porirua Harbour – the next Otaki, the Rev. Hadfield's at the Anglican mission station. Hadfield, who had been ill for a number of years and domiciled in Wellington, had returned to Otaki in the spring of 1849 after almost five years. Sam Williams senior and his wife Mary had stood in for Hadfield during his illness, and would be there until 1854 when they would go to Te Aute, in Hawkes Bay, on Hapuku's Block.

A young Marion Hart who would become Marion Park in 1852. This ambrotype, which was severely damaged, has been digitally reconstructed as closely as possible to an original image. A chance find, it is in the Riccarton House archive. Although ambrotypes date from 1851, an 1856 newspaper advertises this as a new process being practiced in Wellington. On her passport in April 1840 when, at 18, she went with her brother to Paris, she is described as having brown hair and grey eyes. She would be in her early thirties in this photo.

Deans Family Papers, Riccarton Bush Trust.

'Thompson's Warre Otaki ... 1849'.
Te Rauparaha's son Thompson's home,
where Mary Jane and Agnes stayed on
their way to Wanganui in 1852.

C. E. Gold Drawings and Prints B-103-028 A.T.L.

Charlotte Godley (the wife of the Chief Agent for the Canterbury Association, which would establish Christchurch City) who was living in Wellington in 1850 before removing to Lyttleton, describes Otaki which she visited in 1850. Hadfield had 'a little low cottage' built of reeds Maori style and thatched with toitoi, with a sitting room, and two bedrooms, one of which had 'a large french bed with white curtains, carpet all over the floor, quite luxurious,' especially as it had a 'little bathroom' off it. She was the first lady, she said, to have paid Mr Hadfield a visit, and she was made much of. Whether Mr and Mrs Park were invited to stay here in October 1852, his daughter doesn't say, but she does say, they, the girls, spent the night 'as the guest of the Chieftainess'. This would have been Mrs Thompson, the wife of Thompson (Tamihama) Rauparaha, the elder son of old Rauparaha of Ngati Toa who had been so prominent a New Zealand Company adversary at the Wairau and later had promoted the building of the church Rangiatea. Rauparaha had died at Otaki on 27 November 1849.

Either Agnes or her son embroidered the fragments of memory, and had Mrs Thompson brought up in England with her 'own private chapel' at Otaki. This 'chapel' could surely not have been confused with the two-year-old Rangiatea church with its imposing interior, the soaring high pitched roof with ridge pole supported by a central row of single totara tree columns. This was the one 'defect' of the building according to

Mrs Godley (she wanted the conventional two rows of pillars). This church followed the design of the original church at Waikanae.

As for Thompson's wife being brought up in England, this is a mistaken idea. She did in fact have schooling at the Anglican Girls' School in Auckland, and had spent some time at St John's College, with her husband Thompson, and his brother Martin and his wife. They had become committed Christians, and had gone before 1840 to the Bay of Islands to ask for a missionary to be sent to them. The result was Hadfield. Waikanae, at the time the Rauparaha brothers, Thompson and Martin, were urging the church authorities to send a missionary, was still Te Atiawa territory. Otaki, with Te Rauparaha, was Ngati Toa, and although the iwi were related there had been fighting between them. Peace had been made many years before the Parks came through in 1852, when the seat of missionary endeavour had shifted to Otaki. Next to the church was a schoolhouse, in fact a boarding school, and this school and Otaki would have importance to Park's second family. Now, in 1852, with his third love and his first family, he journeyed on to Wanganui.

Marion Park tells of the journey from Otaki to Wanganui. Donald McLean was with the Parks as far as the Manawatu River. Here they spent the night as it was too late for the children to cross. Maori at the ferry provided them with damper, and in an unfinished house in their 'own wrappers passed a capital night'. Next afternoon, reaching the Rangitikei and finding themselves in comfortable quarters they stayed a couple of nights, and on the Monday reached the Turakina where 'the night was passed in a very nice Maori house'. They got to the Wanganui in the early afternoon 'and fortunately crossed the last and most difficult river without accident thanks to the Maories who were driving bullocks and who led the gig across which prevented the necessity of Mr. Park going into the river'. The journey from Wellington to Wanganui had taken a week. It was 'very leisurely out of consideration for the horse and for ourselves'.

The reason why they couldn't initially get lodgings in Wanganui was the dearth of servants. Marion seems to have done the organising of the household largely on her own after they had found a house. Robert was away for a week, and when he returned he had such a severe cold he kept to the house. The Sutherlands had been very kind

The home of the Parks' good friends Captain and Mrs Adams in Wanganui.
R Park. Courtesy David Deans Estate.

to Marion, initiating her into the ways of the place, so different from Wellington. She writes to Susan McLean: 'All the small world here are getting excited and interested in the races which will come off in about a fortnight and really the men must be thankful for something to talk and think about. How they get through the time when the races are passed I cannot imagine for to men there does not seem any means of amusement. We women can find amusement and employment (almost synonymous terms) under any circumstances but for men I pity them.' Marion adds that she is impatient to know

From Duries Hill a good view was had of the growing Wanganui settlement. Above the town were the Blockhouses. Joseph O. Hamley of the 65th Regiment was stationed here in 1853 when the Parks were here. Hamley's wife Martha was aunt to Mary Jane and Agnes. The spire of St Peter's Church is another landmark, close to where Robert Park had bought a section.

R Park. Drawings and Prints A-215-009 A.T.L.

how Susan is as the birth of Susan's first baby is imminent. It is doubtful whether Susan McLean ever read this letter, for following the birth of a baby boy Douglas, Susan died on 7 November 1852. Marion had lost a new and dear friend. But Robert Park had found, through his friendship with the McLeans, an ideal helpmeet, one who was prepared to spend much time on her own, for Robert would be venturing as far across the North Island as Ahuriri (Napier) very soon. The lot of the surveyor's wife.

Wanganui (or Petre as it was officially named until 1853) was still a garrison town, with Colonel Gold and 300 men of the 65th Regiment there. There, also, were Mary Jane and Agnes' Aunt Martha, and her husband Joseph Hamley of the 65th Regiment. There was a certain gaiety about the small town, now peaceful, and Agnes recalled going to her first ball at the age of ten, and of learning all the bugle calls, and enjoying picnics on the Whanganui River. Other good friends of the Park family there were Captain and Mrs Adams, and the Rev. and Mrs Taylor, missionaries at Putiki.

At Putiki, where the main road from Wellington crosses the Whanganui River to enter the town, a boarding school for girls was planned for the mission, where the Rev. Nicholls and his family were to come in 1853. Land was given for the site by Maori owners. The Native Deed of Gift was sent to Governor Grey in the middle of that year. Robert Park was to do the survey which had been arranged by Donald McLean on an earlier visit in 1852. This may have been at the time that McLean, with Park, was at Rangitikei to make the final payment on the Rangitikei purchase. With them was surveyor John Rochfort who was with Park to survey the boundaries of reserves for Maori. He tells of one old chief who, when showing Park the boundaries, pointed to an oven built of stone in a conical shape. 'There' he said exultingly, 'I have roasted my sixteen at once!', meaning of course men, and 'casting at the same time a sidelong look at the said Mr Park's evident bon état, he smacked his lips and grinned'. Park's tendency to portliness is evident in photos taken a few years later. Rochfort was supposed to be going with Park to Hawkes Bay to do further surveys, but as he felt that the government was so stingy with paying him a mere £50 p.a. out of which he had to keep himself and a horse, and pay his travelling expenses, he had decided to give up his 'berth'.

He had, however, sent his instruments by sea to Ahuriri, and as a newcomer to the country, he determined to go on foot from the Manawatu to Hawkes Bay to retrieve them. After nearly freezing to death crossing the Ruahine Range to the 'Ahuriri' plains, he was able to borrow 'the queen's horse' (this was the Queen of Ahuriri, Hapuku's sister) and off

Park's whaleboat drawn up on the shore at Ahuriri (Napier).
R Park. Courtsey David Deans Estate.

he rode to Hapuku's house some 15 miles on. Hapuku, he wrote, 'was a fine well-made man, about six feet in height, and of an intellectual cast of countenance.' Hapuku, he said, had been lately made a magistrate deciding disputes among Maori. Rochfort rode on to the Napier Harbour where he dined with Mr Alexander, the enterprising merchant who had housed McLean and Park on the 1850 visits. The traveller stayed at McCain's Public House on the Western Spit at Ahuriri. There was to have been a wedding there, but Colenso, the Anglican missionary, wouldn't officiate at the hotel so the couple had to travel seven miles through bush to the native church. Colenso was deserving of a lesson, thought Rochfort, and he and an accomplice gave a schooner's seaman a couple bottles of grog to give Colenso a ducking. To satisfy their object they had borrowed Park's five-oared whaleboat at the Harbour. Had Park heard of this episode when he wrote from Wanganui to McLean in that 24 October letter telling of his and his families arrival and in which he gives the 'Ahuriri Memoranda'? It seems that he had thought of making Hawkes Bay his home, and at the very least would be returning to do more surveys there.

McLean had found it slow getting approval from Governor Grey to authorise a survey of the proposed purchase he'd negotiated by January 1852 of blocks running

80 miles down the coast from Hawkes Bay south of Hapuku's (Waipukurau) Block to beyond Castlepoint, and inland to the Ruahine and Tararua Ranges. So Park had left property and gear, including the whaleboat, and 2,000 bricks. Alexander, he says, will take the bricks at original cost, but the whaleboat – 'do not take less than £18' as she is worth £25 and he'd rather rent it to Alexander for his use than sell it below its value. Then there's a medicine chest, £8 Alexander again?, a box of glass – forgets the value but the account is hanging on the wall, locks, soap, tobacco etc., three saddles, a pair of holsters 5/-, some blue shirts and a stretcher that cost 16/-. If they don't sell could they be packed up and sent to Wellington? (by boat). Then he lists 'Things to be sent to Well-. Papers for R Hart – (his new brother-in-law from whose home he has been married). Gun, powder horn etc. Knapsack with papers – Books; all that are in the house'. Small instruments which may have been borrowed by Pelichet, retrieve. 'I should wish the brass parallel be sent down', and all other instruments there, also paper, bill hooks, tent and poles, a black glazed bag and his long boots. Were these the same long boots his daughter Agnes remembered his having in 1847 in Dunedin? He needed to ensure all that was his was returned to him – the government would not recompense him for any loss.

But having settled his family in Wanganui, he was writing to McLean from Ahuriri on 20 December 1852. He sends a tracing of the new piece added to Hapuku's Block and speaks of a dispute between two factions, with Hapuku and the Queen against Park's marking off another area. He has been told by a person of one hapu that if one party was unwilling to sell, he would sell all his interest in the land on the plains to the Crown. Park will not do anything until he hears from McLean, and anyway he's not about to enter squabbles, finding the best policy is to let things alone. It 'works so well' that he is sure he is right. He assumes that as he hasn't heard from him, McLean will have leave of absence for the expected birth. Park has not yet heard of McLean's wife's death and sends his compliments to 'Mrs Mac'. Nobody could have understood better than Robert what his friend McLean would be going through, and when he learned the sad news would have brought back to him the heartbreaking loss he had suffered at the beginning of 1848. Then, his infant son had been stillborn. McLean's boy was alive.

From Napier, in 1851, Robert Park sent shells he had collected to Governor Grey. 'I picked the best for him.' Here are some examples of shells Park is said to have painted.

1947.132.4 Canterbury Museum.

Church windows , possibly St Peters, Wanganui.

R Park FB 67 LINZ Wellington.

Park, having given the 'survey' news to McLean in his December 1852 letter goes blithely on to speak of a visit by Colenso. He concurs here with Rochfort's opinion of the missionary earlier in the year. He had called to look at maps and 'he was d – d civil & it will not go down – ... the look and language of the man is enough to stamp him a Hypocrite he is the third I have met in New Z. of the same stamp and appearance & the other two Stokes of the Gazette & Kettle of Otago I know to be both liars who assume the cloak of godliness for their worldly purposes alone'.

This then was Park with his usual fiery reaction to an unsatisfactory encounter, and consequent attribution of personality and intention to these latter two, his former colleagues, and the unfortunate missionary, who McLean in 1851 had thought well of. This spontaneous reactive form of expression on Park's part would cost him his job in a few years time.

He is afraid his letter and tracing will not get by the *Rose* to Wellington, before McLean has left for Taranaki. 'I have almost forgot that the Queen wishes particularly to have the cap and veil sent up immediately – good that for a present – I suppose she is afraid of her complexion getting spoiled by the sun'. One supposes he is as pleasant to her face as he was to Grey at Foxton at one time. He shouldn't perhaps talk of hypocrisy? There is a P.S. 'I sent the shells direct to the Gov. in case you had left. I picked the best for him'.

In May of 1853 Park is back at Wanganui. He writes to McLean thanking him for his letter of the 13th which enclosed a receipt. This may have been for a down payment on some land at Wanganui which he'd asked McLean to purchase for him back in October 1852. He had two 50-acre blocks in what is now Marybank, above the Putiki Mission Station, and a town lot in Ridgeway Street just below the Queen's Park, where stood St Peters Anglican Church.

Park had told McLean that he would not pay above £30 for a block. In the event his town lot was £50 and the 50 acre lots £40 each, on the three of which he paid a deposit of half the value. His brother-in-law, (by his first wife Mary Anne's sister Martha) Joseph Osbertus Hamley of the 65th, had a bit of a grizzle to his solicitor Strang about the price of a Wanganui town section. He should not pay more than £20 according to Robert Park who had only given £13 for his lot. Which lot? Hamley would write to Robert Hart a few years later, his complaint this time being about his purchase of the lease of a house in 'a most miserable condition'. Should he be paying what he does? After all Colonel Gold's next door had been thoroughly renewed and was 'by far the largest and best situated house in the town' the rent only £60 p.a. Remember Hamley was in Ordnance – he knew about such things. He was, however, to return to Britain with his wife in 1870.

Park doesn't seem to have built anywhere in Wanganui, and he's having regrets about making the town his base, but ruefully writes, 'I am almost sorry I did not go there [Ahuriri] instead of coming here but 'Whatever is, is right' and I will put regrets in my pipe & smoke 'em.' And he asks for Alexander's (Ahuriri) account to be sent him – for the sale of the whaleboat and other goods perhaps?

He knows now, of course, of the sad death of his friend's wife, and that baby Douglas has recently recovered from 'the Flue'. His family, he says, have all had it again, but in a milder way. Which was just as well for poor Marion who was heavily pregnant. It is

Looking down from above Bolton Street and over the Park Cottage roofs to Wakefield's house. Mrs Caroline Abraham, Bishop Abraham's wife, a dear friend of the Parks drew this view in the early 1860s.

Drawings and Prints A-329-009 A.T.L.

to be hoped they had better than those straw beds by the time Robert George Park was born on 18 July 1853.

1854 found the Parks back living in Wellington. Just before Robert had married Marion Hart in September 1852 he had at last received the Crown Grant documents for the land on which Park Cottage stood at the top of Kumutoto Street. It was to here the family probably returned. In the adjoining Bolton Street Cemetery, in April 1853, Marion's mother, also Marion Hart, had been laid to rest.

118

Looking up Bolton Street today. The front driveway to Park Cottage ran in just above the Bolton Hotel. The verger's cottage above is still on the triangle of land Park sold to the church.

Photo Frank Easdale.

In McLean's letter to Park in May 1853 he'd mentioned that the price of everything was very high in Wellington, and that he wished he was living in the Bush as they were. But Robert had replied that at Wanganui their 'only economy is that we do not require to keep so much Coy as you Wellingtonians'. He sends Mrs Park's and his kind regards to McLean and Mr Strang (who had charge of Strang's baby grandson, Douglas Maclean).

Wellington, according to Agnes' memoir, was a pleasant place to be in the 1850s. 'There were lots of excellent maidservants, honest, respectable and loved and respected by their young charges … All the children were dressed in white, and washing was a very big expenditure.' One person loved by Agnes was Bishop Abraham's wife 'and the faith she learned from Bishop Abraham went with her all her days'. It was a tight little community in Wellington and men typically wore many hats, and inevitably were drawn into politics. Park's brothers-in-law, Robert and George Hart, were actively involved, Robert Hart being elected to represent Wellington City in Parliament, and to be law advisor to the Government in Attorney General Swainson's absence. George was elected to the Provincial Council as a Hutt representative. Park attempted to join in. He was appealing in a newspaper in July 1854, to the electors of Wellington. A vacancy had occurred in the Provincial Council and Park offered his services as one of the earliest settlers. As he is personally known to most of them he finds it unnecessary to enter into detailed explanations. He is, he says, a supporter of the present Government and will continue to be so, so long as their policy accords with the liberal institutions they have 'so successfully inaugurated'.

And his 'lengthened experience with regard to the surveys and capabilities of the Waste Lands of the Province will be of practical service in Council'. Should he be elected he could 'with confidence refer to that independence of character which, I trust, has ever distinguished me amongst you, as a guarantee that I shall discharge my public duties in a faithful and liberal spirit'.

In October 1854, he withdraws his offer to stand as a candidate. The Waste Lands after all are to remain in the hands of the General Government instead of being transferred to the Provincial Councils as anticipated. The particular purpose for which he intended to solicit the gentlemen's votes seemed to him 'negatived'. He was, of course, working closely with McLean still, and the development of the Wairarapa purchases was of prime interest. For instance, in December 1854 Donald McLean asks for tenders for a water mill at Papawai in the Wairarapa. Plans and specifications could be seen at the Survey Office on application to Robert Park, Esquire. The policy of setting up water mills for Maori communities to grind wheat had been instituted by Governor Grey.

1854 had not been a kind year with the death of Park's old friend and brother-in-law Richard Baker, who had been married to his first wife's sister Jane Emily at the end of that first hopeful year in Wellington. He was only 44. The prospect of an early death was always a possibility from infancy on. Word, too, would reach him of the death of his only brother Patric, the sculptor, in Manchester on 16 August 1854. Patric was 43. He had helped an old man, taking from him a hamper of ice, and haemorrhaged with the strain. He left a widow, Robina Park, and five children. A 'man of powerful intellect as well as powerful frame', 'a true artist of heroic mould and thought'. Brother Robert might be said to have been cast in a similar mould but in a lesser guise as a younger brother?

Now, back in London, were left only Robert's mother and two sisters, the eldest two Catherine and Agnes, the youngest Eliza having died at 36 in 1852. Catherine the mother would live to be 91, outliving both her sons.

The gravestone at Kensal Green Cemetery London. Robert Park's daughter, mother and sisters all lie here, where Patric Park raised a memorial stone to 'Little Kate', his niece who died in 1840. The inscription to his sister Eliza, who died at 36 in 1852 was added, and after Patric himself died, his sisters Agnes and Catherine inscribed their mother Catherine Lang Park's name following her death in 1876. The eldest daughter Catherine died in 1886 and her sister Agnes in 1890. Agnes' inscription would have been arranged by her sister-in-law, Patric Park's widow, then Mrs Harrison, who was with her at her death.

Courtesy Mairangi Reiher.

CHAPTER 10

A GLIMPSE OF CHRISTCHURCH (1854 – 1861)

For some unknown reason Robert was in Canterbury for a time in 1854.

The chief agent for the Canterbury Association, John Robert Godley, and his wife Charlotte (the recorder of the Otaki visit in 1849 mentioned in Chapter 9) had left New Zealand and the now established town of Christchurch, founded in 1850. The town was not far from those 'Pioneers of the Plains' the Deans of Riccarton. The Deans brothers had been the first settlers on the land in 1843. John Deans had joined his brother William in New Zealand in October 1842. William Deans, it will be recalled, was with Robert Park and the New Zealand Company party who journeyed to Wanganui, and his companion in a boat on the return journey to Wellington.

John and Jane Deans sketched by Robert Park at Riccarton not long before John Deans died in June 1854.

Deans Family Papers, Riccarton Bush Trust.

Sadly, William had been drowned in the total wreck of the *Maria* off Cape Terawhiti in July 1851 as it made to enter Wellington Harbour, en route from Lyttelton to Sydney. John was now on his own, but the farm by 1852, he felt, could support a family of his own. Jane, his love who had had a long wait of seven years back in Scotland, now had a proposal from John, who then returned to Scotland to claim his betrothed. He brought his wife back to Riccarton in February 1853. But John was not well and at the time Robert visited them at their farm and sketched the couple, John was declining noticeably. He died on 23 June 1854. Jane and John had had a short fifteen months together at Riccarton. Their baby John II, born on 6 August 1853, was not yet a year, and would be Jane's only child. Jane never remarried. Robert and Marion Park's son Robert George was of an age with her boy.

It may have been on this trip in 1854 that Robert learned of the establishment of Mrs Maria Thomson's 'Christchurch Ladies School' which had opened in March 1854. But it seems more likely that the possibility of his two older daughters schooling in Christchurch was discussed when Jane Deans paid the Parks a visit when she was in Wellington in 1856 for five weeks. Robert Park and Marion had had another child, a daughter Catherine Edith, born in February 1856. I don't imagine that there was any thought then of the infants, Jane's John and the Parks' Edith, marrying one day; but this is what would be.

On the Wellington visit the Parks and Jane Deans apparently got on well, and in January 1857 all the Parks paid a visit to Riccarton. It was harvest time and Robert was much taken with Bell's Improved Harvester, the first mechanical reaping machine to be used in Canterbury. Jane described Robert (in her *Letters to my Grandchildren*) as being 'quite in ecstasies over it, walking alongside, watch in hand, timing it'. Jane had said she had not been sure about taking them in to stay as she did not have a comfortable room to give them, 'but grandfather [Robert] soon put that right by telling me they had slept under a flax bush'. They did, in fact, all bed down in what was later, in 1886, the day nursery, Robert and Marion, Mary just 15, Agnes 13½, George 3½ and Edith almost two. This day nursery would be filled one day with the many offspring of John and Catherine Edith.

At Robert Hart's in Hobson Street. If it is Marion Park seated with young George beside her and baby Catherine Edith on her knee, the year could have been 1856.

Deans Family Papers, Riccarton Bush Trust.

'Riccarton House from the S.E. 1857', Watercolour R. Park.

Courtesy Patric Deans. (Original pencil sketch in Deans Family Papers Riccarton Bush Trust.)

Riccarton House. Pencil ca 1857, R. Park. Whereabouts at present unknown.

Copied courtesy of the Deans Family from an image in 'Pioneers of the Plains' and with permission of the author, Gordon Ogilvie.

Photograph of a painting of Riccarton House between 1863 and 1870. The whereabouts of the original watercolour are at present unknown.

It was a successful visit. They had 'such jolly evenings, songs all round and as many as could would sing'. (Robert was renowned for his fine singing voice.) 'We had only the parlour for meals, but it was quite wonderful how elastic it was, and how good-naturedly people took what they got in those days.' All did their own bedrooms, Jane did the cooking, Marion Park and Mrs Eaglesome helped wash up and generally. It seems likely that it was at this time that the girls Mary Jane 15 and Agnes 13½, were left at Mrs Thomson's 'Avon House' to be 'finished', the arrangements having been made the previous year. They would, according to Agnes, spend school breaks at the Deans or with surveyor Cass and his family, and with Dr and Mrs Fisher. They probably spent the long summer break back in Wellington, as Agnes speaks of once when the monthly steamer *Zingari*, which plied between Wellington and Lyttelton, was delayed, Robert sailed with his daughters in the cutter *Salopian*. On board this vessel was the Hon. George Buckley. This is likely to have been when Robert made application on

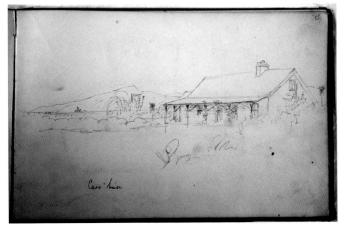

Left: Surveyor Cass' house where Mary Jane and Agnes would sometimes stay in the holidays when they were not at the Deans or at Dr. Fisher's. Pencil, ca 1862.

R Park 1972.123.15 Canterbury Museum.

Below: 'Christchurch & plains' from Casterton. The view that the Parks would have had also had they built on the Bridle Path Road. Riccarton Bush can be seen in the distance.

R Park 1972.123.14 Canterbury Museum.

The 50-acre block today, with the northern and southern bounds indicated approximately by arrows. Now extensively built upon from the Bridle Path Road frontage along the Heathcote River to just beyond the Ferrymead Historic Homestead of the original ferry crossing on the right, and up to Major Hornbrook Road on the top ridge with sweeping views including the ocean to the east. The Ferrymead Bridge to Sumner lies just to the left.

Photo Frank Easdale.

'Casterton & bridle path' along from the 50 acres which Robert Park purchased in 1858.

R Park 1972.123.27 Canterbury Museum.

4 March 1858 to purchase 50 acres above the Heathcote ferry on the Bridle Track Road. An attractive property commanding a view over the Estuary, north up the coast to Kaikoura, and west across Christchurch town and over the Canterbury Plains to the Southern Alps. He received the Crown Grant in July 1858. The Hon. George Buckley, later to be manager of the Bank of New Zealand, in 1876, when living in the Heathcote Valley, bought this 50-acre block on which Park had never built. Is it possible that in 1858 Park was then thinking of making a move south from Wellington, or was the purchase merely speculation?

For the moment, though, Park was much occupied with Wellington affairs and with his position as Chief Surveyor of the Wellington Province. There was always pressure on the Survey Department, with purchasers clamouring to have their boundaries defined, particularly in the Wairarapa. Here the waste lands had come under the new 5/- an acre scheme in 1858. Featherston, the Superintendent of the Province, wished to fill the depleted coffers of Wellington by having 100,000 to 200,000 acres available for purchase yearly. This was a bone of contention with Robert Park who disputed with Featherston, and Fitzherbert, the Commissioner of Crown Lands, the policy of doing quick surveys for this 5/- acreage. Not only did it offend his professional sensibility but he damned it as uneconomic. In one letter to the Superintendent he writes: 'You know that with him and your Honor I have remonstrated and at last protested against the sacrifice of the effective strength of the (survey) office to the rough surveys of land to be offered for sale at 5/- an acre; your reply being that so urgent with the Government of this Province is the need for money, that all progress toward the completion of the surveys of land already sold, must give way before these rough surveys (not withstanding I pointed out to you the greatly increased cost, and waste of this mode of proceeding).' He hears that the Land Office gives as reason for delays in the issue of Crown Grants, that the stoppage was in the Survey Department. 'Your Honor's statement 'that you have been painfully aware of the unsatisfactory state of the Survey department' gives colour to the implied charge which only those acquainted with the facts of the case know to be unfounded'. The epistle concludes 'I shall have failed in the object of this letter if I have not conveyed to your Honor my strong conviction that the repeated interference of your Honor and the Land Commissioner (Fitzherbert) with the work and staff of the Survey Office has been such as to weaken and almost destroy its efficiency.

George Swainson, District Surveyor in Wellinton in 1860.

R Park. Courtesy David Deans Estate.

I cannot conclude without thanking your Honor for giving me the opportunity of meeting charges which I hear have been insinuated by others but never been openly brought forward.

I remain Sir

Your obedient servant.'

This last sarcastic sentence of Park's and the 'tone and spirit' of the letter were too much for Featherston who had been disputing with Park through a series of letters from April 1860, a matter which was ultimately to trigger Park's dismissal as Chief Surveyor of the Wellington Province. Park and Featherston were of opposing political persuasions, and, according to Park, Featherston in his position as Superintendent of the Province over two years had become 'a complete Tyrant and no one under him has the slightest chance of getting on with him unless he eats dirt by the bushel'. This is exactly what Surveyor Swainson, the person at the centre of this dispute, the trigger, had been compelled to do, wrote Park.

The dispute had begun in April when by letter Park was asked by Featherston to direct Mr Swainson to survey 'the 5/- lands commencing with the blocks in Mr Riddiford's run' in the Wairarapa. Park replied that Swainson could start the following week but as he has been drawn for Militia, it would be necessary to find a substitute for him, as it was unlikely that Major Trafford would grant Swainson two months leave of absence'. He suggests that Mr Clarke could do it. There was considerable alarm at this time, April 1860, in the light of fighting between Maori and Pakeha in Taranaki over the Waitara purchase. Would hostilities break out too between the Wairarapa tribes and the settlers? Featherston had been reassured by the Colonial Secretary on 23 April that it was most unlikely that there were grounds for alarm. Further a large meeting at Papawai Marae (the site of a Grey water mill) would indicate that the Wairarapa Maori had no wish to clash with Pakeha. But Major Trafford insisted on calling the Wellington militia to parade 'for exercise and training' in the Hutt. Park felt that militia parade requirements could be 'harmonised' with survey needs in the service of the public.

Backwards and forwards went the dispute, Park maintaining what he perceived as the autonomy of his position, by directing Swainson; Featherston demanding that his wishes should be obeyed, and fuming when they were not. The culmination came when Swainson was asked to resign. Unfair! cried both Swainson and Park, Swainson protesting that he acted as usual on Park's instructions, Park agreeing that he had given these. But then, for District Surveyor Swainson 'through the intercession of friends' (wrote Park in a personal letter to McLean in July 1860 after both he and Swainson had been dismissed) 'a door was opened . . . by allowing him to apologise and to "coincide" with His Honor that the two berths 'district Surveyor' & 'Militia officer' were incompatible'. The truth was that had both left the Survey Office there was no one in the office to get up the 5/- land maps, consequently 'his Honor was likewise glad of the chance of taking Swainson back until that work was accomplished when he had better watch out'. With this bitter letter, Park forwarded to McLean a copy of the letter of dismissal dated 29 June which said 'that from and after this day, I dispense with your services as Principal Surveyor of this Province' and was signed by Featherston.

The Wairarapa Maori in the end had not supported, by rebellion, the Taranaki disturbances, despite the rumours which had reached Maori ears that 'Wideawake' Edward Jerningham Wakefield had boasted that 3000 soldiers were coming to crush the Maori. Featherston was able to squash this rumour, and therefore felt justified in his attitude to Swainson. Whether he was justified in attempting to override Park's directions is another matter.

Now Robert was out of work. He had family to support, a wife and five children, with his two eldest daughters at boarding school in Christchurch, and a social position to uphold. He needed a job and knew McLean would do what he could for him. What would suit him best, he told 'Mac', would be 'a small retiring pension & allowed to do private work'. Four days later he's writing again. He's had further misfortune. He's found that at a time he was away in Canterbury he had his commission in the militia reduced, according to the *Gazette*, from Captain to Lieutenant, with a consequent loss of pay. He has, he protests, never resigned his command. Others had been made Captains, one of whom was Will Bannatyne who had never served the battalion at all. (Bannatyne had married Richard Baker's widow Jane Emily, Robert Park's first wife's sister. There was no personal falling out with Bannatyne. The Bannatynes would remain very closely associated with the Parks in

Above: Young George, the first-born of Robert and Marion, looks to be about five in this photo. The photo is likely to have been taken outside the door of Park Cottage ca 1858.

Above left and left: Robert Park with his daughters Mary Jane and Agnes. Again probably taken outside the door to their home in Wellington.

Above: The girls in 1858 would be 16 and 14 and perhaps home on holiday from Mrs Thomson's school in Christchurch.

Crawford Album Photographic Coll. A.T.L. PA1-f-019-23

Left. Robert Park with Agnes.

Riccarton Bush Trust

Photos taken in Hobson Street Wellington ca 1859.

Left: Robert Park with Mrs. Jessie Crawford whose husband James Crawford possibly took the photograph.

Crawford Album Photographic Coll. PA1-019-18-3 A.T.L.

Below: Mrs Bannatyne, who is standing, is Mary Anne Park's sister Emily Jane. She was the widow of Major Baker. Seated is Mrs Caroline Abraham, wife of Bishop Abraham.

Crawford Album Photographic Coll. PA1-f-019-25-3 A.T.L.

133

'The Wreck of the *Tyne*', sketched by Park two days after the *Tyne* was wrecked at Sinclair Head on 6 July 1845 showing a rig devised to bring goods ashore. Park has fixed the position of the wreck in this sketch.

Courtesy David Deans Estate.

the future.) Park harked back 15 years to the wreck of the *Tyne* when he was a Lieutenant in the W Battalion. He received public thanks for his conduct at the time, 'the only officer who did – I do not write this boastfully but merely to shew that upon that account I had some claim'. Could McLean put in a word in the right quarter? He will recollect that it was because he accepted a command in the Militia that he lost his civil situation – 'rather hard to be now done out of both … the Governor [Gore Browne] could save me.'

He must have been at a low, so soon after being dismissed, but by November, characteristically, he has some fight back. To 'Mac' he writes thanking for his kindness in thinking of a berth that would suit him. He is 'at present a candidate for the General Assembly along with Wakefield & Bowler a bad lot I hear you say but these were the only two to come forward'. Weld, they have since found was a possibility but it was too late now. He didn't think there was much chance for their 'triumvirate'. Park had been told that his name had had 'a capital reception' at a public meeting, much to Feathertston's chagrin as he had arranged the meeting to report his own party's doings. Now Featherston's party was spreading reports injurious to Park's character – that he was never at the Office – never did anything – and that he had 'received a wigging' from the Auckland Government for his behaviour to the Superintendent. Wakefield too was in bad repute and had quarrelled with Stokes & Hunter. (This last was not surprising.) He will put a short plain statement, in the *Advertiser*, tomorrow of the circumstances of his dismissal. He goes on to relate a hoax played on McLean's elderly father-in-law, Robert Strang, condems the perpetrators, and then reverts to his concern about a berth that McLean has evidently thought of.

He is, he writes, getting tired of running about the country, would prefer something stationary, even with less pay, and to be allowed to do private work of which he should get a sufficiency. For instance he might be a surveyor of Native Reserves about Wellington. 'But I must be entirely from under the control of the Provincial Governt. I don't think I could ever serve under Featherston again or any Provincialist. The Featherston party have been throwing out baits for me but the fishers are too clumsy and the hook is too distinct & the bait is nasty.' For instance, a 'friend' says 'Does Park ever go to Browns now?' It is hinted that should he meet Commissioner Fitzherbert there the rift might be mended. No apology – just a mutual forgetfulness. This was a ploy to make him seek the meeting. If it didn't work he sees he could be jeered at. 'No! had Featherston done and acted like a gentleman at the commencement no disagreement might have taken place.' Then comes the angry letter damming Featherston as a 'Tyrant'.

In December he's writing to McLean again. It's no surprise to him that he hasn't been elected nor either of the other 'Radicals'. 'Bribery and corruption were at work but so well managed that we cannot lay our hands upon a good case as yet.' Featherston had not made amends though Park had heard he was very sorry.

In his December letter, Park is not so adamant about travelling. He has been considering the matter and concludes 'that any situation under the Imperial Governt. is preferable to one either General or Provincial Govt. and I presume that would be the case with a berth connected with the Native Surveys. The Home Govt. are not likely to give up the Native management to any Colonial Legislature until at least peace is firmly established.' So if 'Mac' can procure him employment with his department he should 'feel both happy & oblige'. His wishes seem to have been satisfied as in April 1861 he is back from Ahuriri (Napier) and has got 'Mac's' letter 'anent the N. Reserve on the Tinakori Rd'. In Hawkes Bay he had been looking at the boundaries of purchases of further blocks from the Crown

'Woodburn Ruataniwha.'
So aptly named is the
homestead with this yet
desolate view. Park was
surveying here in 1861.

R Park. Courtesy David Deans Estate.

to add to McLean's Maraekakaho pastoral run. McLean had his brothers Alexander and Archibald running this, but by 1863 McLean himself would be largely living in Hawkes Bay. He relinquished his position as Native Secretary to take over the duties of Superintendent of Hawkes Bay, as well as being the Government Native Agent for the East Coast. McLean's brothers Archibald and Alexander, had come to New Zealand in 1858 and 1861 respectively. McLean's sisters Catherine and Annabella were with their brothers at Maraekakaho where they would later care for their motherless nephew Douglas who had been in Grandfather Strang's charge. Park reported to 'Mac' on Maraekakaho – 'All your folks are well the ladies have made a great change in the appearance of the house by papering, carpentering etc'.

Park ends by commenting that he does not like 'the report that … peace has been established with the natives, they have not had a sufficient lesson yet. I also hope that your heeland friend Cameron will walk into them'. Park could perhaps see his position with McLean disappearing. What he couldn't see was that the natives that might be walked into would include his and Terenui's son, Huta Pamariki Park. A son he has perhaps had no knowledge of. Certainly he had never known of his son's or his daughter Anihaka's whereabouts after Huta's birth in December 1850.

CHAPTER 11

ANIHAKA & HUTA PARK – THE SECOND FAMILY 1850 – 1868

The memories of Anihaka and Huta, Robert Park's two children by Terenui, were conditioned by what they had been told by their Maori relatives.

They never knew their Pakeha father, nor heard stories of him from Terenui who had died at Huta's birth. What they could be sure of was their Maori heritage.

Te Atiawa descend from a common ancestor Te Whiti o Rongomai I. In the 1820s and the 1830s this tribe was living around Ngamotu Beach (on the present New Plymouth foreshore). Here they welcomed the seamen and flax traders Jacky Love and Dick Barrett, both of whom took Maori 'wives'. A descendant of Jacky Love would, in years to come, take as a wife a granddaughter of Robert Park and Terenui. This granddaughter would be Te Atiawa and marry a distant cousin descended from Te Puni, also Te Atiawa.

The Chiefs Te Puni and Wharepouri (who would negotiate with the New Zealand Company) were at Ngamotu when the tribes to their north came down upon them. Earlier, Te Atiawa's allies Ngati Toa were to the north in Kawhia. Next to them were the Waikato tribes of Tainui and Ngati Maniapoto. Rauparaha of Ngati Toa, the principal fighting chief at Kawhia, knew that these powerful and covetous neighbours could conquer and destroy Ngati Toa. At Rauparaha's behest a southward migration began, to the Kapiti Coast and the top of the South Island. Te Atiawa, too, were anxious about their hold on their ancestral lands in Taranaki. Some were following Ngati Toa's example and going south. In December 1831 the Waikato tribes advanced inexorably on, slaughtering or enslaving hundreds. Of those that escaped, several hundred sought protection from the friendly Ngati Ruanui tribe around the coast south of Mt Taranaki, while others moved down to the Kapiti Coast to establish a Te Atiawa enclave at Waikanae (near Otaki where Ngati Toa with Rauparaha were strong). Among those gone south had been the chief Ngata-ta-i-te-Rangi. Now, in the face of an attack on their homeland,

Honiana Te Puni. A photo of the painting which once hung in the reception room in Ripeka and Wi Hapi Love's home Taumata, in Petone.

[C.H.Barraud]. Courtesy Peter Love.

Ngatata and his son, Wi Tako Ngatata, had returned to Taranaki. Tainui came down upon the the Pā at Ngamotu. By a ruse Te Atiawa, with Love and Barrett taking part in the defence, triumphed. For a period there was a short uneasy peace when bartering actually went on between the 'enemies'. Te Wherowhero, the Waikato (Tainui) chief, who would become the first Maori King in 1858, decided to return to the Waikato. But first he let those in the Pā know he would mount a last assault. And so he did, was repulsed, then retreated north. Te Atiawa knew that it was a hollow victory for them and it would only be a matter of time when utu would be taken.

There would have to be a mass exodus to the south, where they would get guns, rally those already there, and return. Te Puni and Wharepouri led some 1,400 warriors and as many elders, women and children, leaving behind a small number of the tribe to keep the land warm assuring continuity of ownership. Love and Barrett went south with them. This was June 1832. It was February 1833 before they reached Waikanae (Te Uruhi). There had been a battle on the way with the Taupo chief Te Heuheu, who, surprisingly, was routed, but this affray had meant considerable delay as well as loss of life.

Barrett and Love, after a time on the Kapiti Coast, moved across Cook Strait accompanied by a number of Te Atiawa and joined Jacky Guard the whaler at Te Awaiti on Arapawa Island in the Marlborough Sounds, again under the dominance of the increasingly powerful Rauparaha. Here, no longer flax traders, they became whalers. Arapawa was well populated with Te Atiawa, mainly around East Bay, some of whom had been around for a number of years having previously joined with Rauparaha in his southern incursions into Ngai Tahu territory in the South Island, fighting battles with him at Kaiapoi (north of Christchurch) and Akaroa on Banks Peninsula. In 1834 Ngai Tahu retaliated with an attack on the Ngati Toa in the Sounds. Rauparaha was away to their frustration. In 1838 Rauparaha went south to confront the Ngai Tahu taua, again bent on exacting utu. A truce was eventually called.

The traders turned whalers, Barrett and Love, had found it increasingly hard to make a living at whaling. Many more stations had been established and American whalers now operated about Cloudy Bay and the Sounds. All would soon change. The New Zealand Company's ship *Tory* with the Wakefields was on its way, and Barrett would be with them as they sailed up and down the west coast of the North Island and into Wellington Harbour, when Barrett played a large part as an interpreter negotiating the initially absurdly large areas to be purchased. His relationship with the Wellington chiefs through living with, fighting alongside, and marrying into the tribe and his knowledge of the language made him invaluable at this time. Jacky Love, however was not to be with them. He had died at Te Awaiti in 1839, a half canoe raised as a traditional memorial.

Hohepine Ngatata and her husband Taniora Love.
Courtesy Peter Love.

But from the doughty John Agar (Jacky) Love's union with Mereruru Te Hikanui came Hone Tanerau, and then the grandson Taniora (Daniel Mana Love) who would marry Te Amo (Hohepine) Ngatata (only daughter of Wi Tako Ngatata). From this marriage, Wi Hapi Love was born. The circle was complete with the marriage of Wi Hapi to Ripeka Matene, Ripeka being the daughter of Anihaka Park (and Patrick Matene/Tauwhare, a grandson of Te Puni), and granddaughter of surveyor Robert Park and Terenui (who was a cousin of Wi Tako Ngatata).

The Maori relationships are complicated, with multiple marriages and overlapping generations. To Huta Pamariki Park and his sister Anihaka, Wi Tako Ngatata appears to be a first cousin of their mother, Terenui, but was called an uncle. Another uncle, or great-uncle, of Huta and Anihaka was Titokowaru, of the South Taranaki tribe Ngati Ruanui. Titokowaru was apparently related to Huta and Anihaka through Whetowheto, Ngatata-i-te-Rangi's first wife, also of Ngati Ruanui, who was Wi Tako Ngatata's mother. An abbreviated whakapapa setting out some of these relationships is at the end of this chapter.

The early years of Park's two children by Terenui, his second family, are shadowy. There are half a dozen variations told by descendants of events following Huta Pamariki Park's birth in December 1850. Two stories are consistent. That Anihaka went to an aunt in Otago, and Huta to an uncle in Taranaki. But from where, and when they went, differs.

Huta's son Harry Park would write in 1939, that Terenui had died at Pipitea Pā in Wellington. Perhaps. All that remained of the old Pipitea Pā in 1850 were a few derelict whare, but there were hints of revival with a new church being built. Nearby, though,

Wi Tako Ngatata. A photo of the painting originally in the house Taumata.

Courtesy Peter Love.

were many weatherboard houses which Maori had built for themselves. The chief of Pipitea and nearby Kumutoto Pā, Wi Tako Ngatata, whose house became the police station, had moved to Ngauranga. Harry Park has it that Hone Kitakita (Te Tupe) went to the Pā with a dray and a wooden box for a coffin, took Terenui and buried her at the Maori cemetery in Te Puni Street, Petone. Kitakita was a 'hard man' wrote Harry, and overrode the tribal feelings which had, he said, caused Terenui to be ostracised. This 'hard man' would become Huta's father-in-law.

When Robert Park returned from surveying up country, continues Harry, he found Terenui had died and his children by her gone. He 'searched in vain' for them. Anihaka's daughter Ripeka Love heard it differently. Robert had gone back to Scotland. On returning it was the same story; he found the children had been spirited away. However, the reason given by Ripeka was that the children's Maori relatives were apprehensive as they had heard it was Robert's intention to take his second family's children (presumably along with the first family's two, Mary Jane and Agnes, though they are never mentioned because Harry Park has them drowned in Sydney Harbour) back to Scotland to be educated. They might never come back. Harry says further that Robert gave Wi Tako Ngatata £100 for each of the children and 100 acres of land in trust, with the exhortation, 'Above all have them educated'. (The latter he certainly did not do – the money? well he could have given Terenui or Wi Tako money previously, but as a settlement on them? – I don't believe so. In fact it is uncertain if he was even aware

Pipitea Pā in 1841. Part 6 of a Panorama by George Hilliard. By 1850, when Terenui died, any old whare left were derelict and Maori had built themselves European style houses nearby.

Drawings and Prints C-012-005-6 A.T.L.

he had a son.) There is a story, too, which other descendants of Huta in Nelson have, that Terenui's uncle Titokowaru carved a coffin for Terenui. This seems unlikely – there would have been too short a time between word of her unexpected death to have reached him before her burial. He was a Maori missioner at Patea at the time.

Here then, was an infant needing a wet nurse, and a tiny girl under two years. Huta wouldn't have been sent off to the mission school at Otaki right then as Harry seems to indicate. In any event, the boarding school did not come into being until 1852. That Anihaka, as Harry writes, went to an aunt in Otago is so, but not until she was about eight years old according to Ripeka – after also going to the mission boarding school at Otaki. They both might indeed have been there for a time, but unfortunately no list of pupils has been found. Neither are there any reports of the convenient fire alleged by Harry Park to have destroyed the records of Robert and Terenui's marriage by the Rev. Hadfield. No marriage lines have been found, and at the time a marriage was supposed to have taken place, Hadfield was not officiating as a priest as he was unwell for some years.

'Mission Station at Otaki ... 1853.' Both Anihaka and Huta Park are said to have been at the Mission School here which began in 1852.

Janetta Maria Cookson. Drawings and Prints A-048-043 A.T.L.

Harry Park's 1939 tale of Huta's going to his great-uncle Titokowaru in Taranaki is an interesting one. As a youngster at Otaki, Huta one day followed Hakopa (a mission worker, and possibly the man later named as a 'lieutenant' of Titokowaru) along the beach north. Hakopa was heading for Taranaki. Coming to a river Hakopa became aware that the boy had followed him. So Hakopa took him along with him, and from then, until he was about 18, he was with his uncle Titokowaru, and raised in old Maori tradition.

Huta's sister Anihaka, daughter Ripeka says, went to her aunt in Otago from the Otaki mission school. (Perhaps missing his sister had caused the six to seven year old to follow Hakopa?) Anihaka's Te Atiawa aunt Koraraina (Caroline) married the southern paramount Ngai Tahu chief, Te Matenga Taiaroa, in April 1858, the same day that he was baptised into the Methodist Church on the marae at Taiaroa Heads. She was his third wife (or possibly fourth?) Anihaka would have been about ten then. It is quite possible she had accompanied her aunt south earlier and that Taiaroa and Koraraina had been together before the union was blessed by the church. Peace had long been made between Ngai Tahu and Te Atiawa and Ngati Toa (Rauparaha and Rangihaeata's tribe). Taiaroa had indeed travelled north to Porirua as far back as 1843; an earnest of goodwill.

Leaving Anihaka in the care of her aunt, we can return to Huta. It could have been about 1856-57 when Huta became a ward of his uncle Titokowaru. By then Titoko, who had been a mission worker, had turned his back on missionary Christianity and become part of the Maori nationalist movement with its

Left: Koraraina Taiaroa, Anihaka's aunt, who was a daughter of Ngatata-i-te-rangi, and related through one of her father's wives to Titokowaru of Taranaki. Huta would spend his young manhood with Titoko.

Courtesy Peter Love.

Redoubt at Sentry Hill (Bell Block) in 1865 drawn by surveyor S. Percy Smith.

FB W1 LINZ, New Plymouth.

The often-reproduced lithograph of a painting by Kennett Watkins of the death of von Tempsky at Te Ngutu-o-te-Manu. Huta is said to have seen him shot from up a tree. Perhaps he was one of those shown here in the towering tree on the left.

Drawings and Prints C-033-006 A.T.L.

proposals to elect a Maori king and its opposition to land sales. Titokowaru's name may have been suggested for the kingly role showing he had much mana already with the gathered tribal representatives at Pukawa on the shores of Lake Taupo in 1858. In the 1860-61 Taranaki War against Pakeha over land purchases he was likely (according to his biographer James Belich) to have led a raiding party who had killed Captain King near New Plymouth in February 1861. His prowess as a warrior, tactician and engineer of defences was being honed. Young Huta, then aged ten, would not have been part of this nor of the Waikato war of 1863-64 where, in North Taranaki in the failed attack on Te Manere, Titokowaru lost an eye at Sentry Hill. He may have helped his uncle in the defence of his home at Pungarehu in late 1866 when he would have been 16. Titokowaru was on the rise and the mantle of the prophet Te Ua who died in 1866 had slipped easily around his shoulders. He had rebuilt the village of Te Ngutu-o-te-manu, The Beak of the Bird, at Pungarehu. Then began Titoko's peace campaign with many peace meetings, his religion having perhaps a stronger base of Christianity than that of his famous contemporary Te Whiti-o-Rongomai III at Parihaka. Five peace meetings were held at Te Ngutu-o-te-manu, with its 58 houses, its marae, and its 'beautiful meeting house Wharekura'. Did Huta go on the peace march in June and July of 1867 which went from Taranaki to Wanganui and up the river to Pipiriki? Very probably.

But the 'creeping confiscation' of the Pakeha authorities became too much, despite Titokowaru's urging of non-violent resistance to this loss of ancestral lands. When Huta was 17 in the middle of 1868 conflict broke out again. Now Titoko actively opposed the confiscations, and apparently on his orders three military settlers were killed on disputed land. Punitive raids were made by the military on Te Ngutu-o-te-manu. Rather than give up one escapee who had sought refuge with him Titoko went

Titokowaru on the left as an old man with Te Whiti on trial in Wellington. Detail from sketches by W J Leslie in a supplement to the *Evening Press* 8 October 1886.

Drawings and Prints B-034-015 A.T.L.

to war. There were five campaigns from June 1868 to March 1869. He and his followers were victorious in these battles, and it was at Te Ngutu-o-te manu when a colonist force was destroyed that their leader, the colourful and brave von Tempsky, was killed. Family legend has it that 18-year-old Huta was in a tree and saw von Tempsky fall and die.

At another time Huta is said to have taken food to his uncle who was sheltering under a church. This may have been after Titoko had abandoned his fortification at Tauranga-ka, near Waitotara. His army was disintegrating, his mana declining (for Maori political reasons) and he lost his war. Later he would come to an understanding with the government, rebuild villages, and form a closer alliance with Te Whiti and Tohu of Parihaka. He was imprisoned three times, and although unwell in 1885 and 1886 he was then looking to peaceful reconciliation once more. Titokowaru died in August 1888. He was buried secretly. The final resting place of his bones is said to be known only by Huta Park descendants. None of Titoko's trials would immediately affect Huta who in about 1869 set off for Otakou to find his long lost sister Anihaka.

This canoe prow Tauihu, from the waka of Wi Hapi Pakau was also once in Taumata. It is now held in Te Papa Tongarewa. Two views of the prow are shown, fore and aft.

Courtesy Peter Love.

This canoe prow symbolises the Te Atiawa relationship of people in Robert Park's Maori family through his union with Terenui. The canoe prow, known as Tauihu, was from the personal waka of Wi Hapi Pakau. Wi Hapi Pakau, appears to have lived for a time at Kumutoto Pā which had been established in 1824 by Pomare and Ngatata-i-te-Rangi (his uncle). In 1835 Pomare and others left for the Chatham Islands. Wi Hapi Pakau was again for a time at Kumutoto Pā in 1836. In 1844 there were only two signatures on the Deed of Release for the land about Kumutoto Pā: Wi Tako Ngatata, whose father Ngatata-i-te-Rangi had put his chiefly cloak around his son's shoulders in 1842, and the tohunga Wi Hapi Pakau.

Much later Wi Tako Ngatata and his second wife Mere Te Hamene had a daughter Te Amo (Hohepine/Josephine) who married Taniora (Daniel) Love. They in turn had a son who was named Wi Hapi Pakau Love for his venerable cousin. Wi Hape Pakau was a chief mourner at his cousin Wi Tako Ngatata's funeral in 1887. Alongside him was his five-year-old namesake Wi Hapi Pakau Love. Wi Hape Pakau died in 1897, a very old man of 100 years. Wi Hapi Pakau Love inherited the canoe prow.

Peter Love, a grandson of Ripeka and Wi Hapi Pakau Love, could be said to have known the canoe prow intimately when it was in the Hall, used as a Marae, in the Love home Taumata in Petone. Peter, his brother Michael, and other small cousins had much delight in 'riding' as a rocking horse, this waka prow.

Today, this canoe prow, now restored, is a treasure held at the Museum of New Zealand Te Papa Tongarewa.

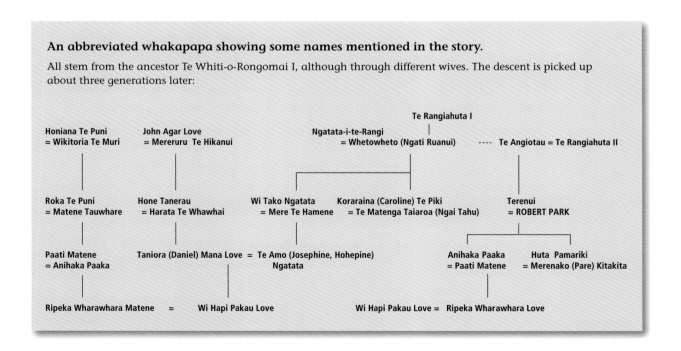

An abbreviated whakapapa showing some names mentioned in the story.

All stem from the ancestor Te Whiti-o-Rongomai I, although through different wives. The descent is picked up about three generations later:

Te Rangiahuta I

Honiana Te Puni = Wikitoria Te Muri

John Agar Love = Mereruru Te Hikanui

Ngatata-i-te-Rangi = Whetowheto (Ngati Ruanui)

---- Te Angiotau = Te Rangiahuta II

Roka Te Puni = Matene Tauwhare

Hone Tanerau = Harata Te Whawhai

Wi Tako Ngatata = Mere Te Hamene

Koraraina (Caroline) Te Piki = Te Matenga Taiaroa (Ngai Tahu)

Terenui = ROBERT PARK

Paati Matene = Anihaka Paaka

Taniora (Daniel) Mana Love = Te Amo (Josephine, Hohepine) Ngatata

Anihaka Paaka = Paati Matene

Huta Pamariki = Merenako (Pare) Kitakita

Ripeka Wharawhara Matene = Wi Hapi Pakau Love

Wi Hapi Pakau Love = Ripeka Wharawhara Love

CHAPTER 12

TO CANTERBURY – A NEW LIFE, 1861 – 1870

When Huta left Taranaki for Otago in about 1869, Robert Park had been well-settled on the sheep run Winchmore, sub-leased from his brother-in-law George Hart, since at least 1862.

Before leaving Wellington he had seen his eldest daughter Mary Jane (then 19) safely married to John Gibson Kinross. The Scot Kinross, was, when he married Mary, a well-established and well-liked merchant in Napier. He had arrived in Wellington in 1846 and had ventured into the purchase of sheep runs in Hawkes Bay. He was the Napier agent for Donald McLean and instrumental in McLean's purchase of the Maraekakaho land where McLean's two sisters, Annabella, and Catherine (Kate) who married solicitor Robert Hart, were to come in 1861. A friendship naturally expanded between the two families which had also embraced Robert Park. The Harts had Scottish links through their mother's family. The Scottish inheritance was pivotal to the relationships and remained so. Even when Kinross was bankrupted following the failure of a Scottish bank, in the slump of 1870, McLean retained Kinross as his agent.

The bride and her family, on the day of the wedding, 19 September 1861, given a fine day, might easily have walked from Park Cottage the short distance to the first St Paul's Church reached from Kumutoto Street (Museum Street did not exist at that date). Here the Bishop of Wellington, Bishop Abraham, assisted by his curate (a former

The view from Bolton Street (above Park Cottage, the roofs of which are seen below the picket fence). The original St Paul's Church where Mary Jane Park was married in 1861 is to right of centre a short distance from the Parks' home.

Photographic Coll. 031742 A.T.L.

architect and designer of 'Selwyn' churches) the Rev. Fredrick Thatcher, solemnised the union. Mary no doubt felt doubly blessed to be married by Bishop Abraham as she probably felt, along with her sister Agnes, that 'the faith she had learned from Bishop Abraham went with her all her days'. Agnes was a witness to the signing of the register. The Kinrosses made their home in Napier at Mount Alloway.

Agnes, at about 18, when the move was made to Canterbury, would probably have left Mrs Thomson's school in Christchurch. Her role may now have been to assist her stepmother Marion in the care of her half-brother Robert George (called George) then nine and his sisters Catherine Edith six, and Elizabeth Marion four, and help with numerous and endless household tasks.

A view across the plains to Mt Hutt from Winchmore 1869. One of Park's last paintings, which hangs in William Dean's home, Morven, part of the original Homebush estate of the Deans family.
Courtesy David Deans Estate.

Robert, when not supervising the running of the station, was surveying for the Provincial Government. In 1862 he undertook two looping traverses, surveying from the flagpole at Winchmore on the Ashburton River, taking sights on Mount Somers and Mount Alford, sketching and describing as he surveyed, the terrain, the stations, and the names of runholders in his field books, going on by way of the Stour River to Lake Heron and on to the confluence of the Rakaia and Mathias Rivers, setting up camp near Double Hill. A tragedy was to happen on the Rakaia. Park is said to have sent a cadet from here with some letters to take back to Winchmore. After a week the cadet had not returned and on enquiring at Gray's Run it was found he had not stayed overnight there as expected. Gray's men searched but saw no sign of the young man. A week after he had been missed one of Gray's shepherds chanced upon the lad's body at the bottom of a steep bank to the Rakaia. Near him lay his pocket book, the last lines in his diary almost illegible, but 'thirsty' and 'water' could be made out. He had broken his leg, the bank was too steep to climb, the roar of the river would have muffled any cries for help – had a rare horseman have passed by. He died trying to get to the river to drink. There is another version of this sad accident told to Austen Deans by his grandmother Catherine Edith Deans, Robert Park's daughter. In this the cadet was taking a route on the south side of Lake Coleridge, when his horse fell and broke its leg pinning him beneath. They died together, and of an evening now when it is going to snow, if one is near the spot, the cries of the helpless lad can be heard above the river's roar.

Park perforce continued on with his traverse, up the Wilberforce to the streams Moa and Kiwi and Big Goat Hill where he would have looked across to (but does not mention) Major Scott's run Glenthorne, though he notes the Harper River and Lake Selfe. Down then to Oakden's run between Lake Coleridge and the Rakaia River, taking sights on Fighting Hill, Mount Hutt, and Pudding Hill, and so back by Alford Forest to Winchmore.

The Alford Forest area must have appealed to him, for on 3 April 1862 he applied to purchase 20 acres there. The block (on McFarlans Road) is described in the application as being 'Alford Forest to the northward of the single tree & about one quarter of a mile north of land belonging to William Thomas'. A rather better defined Crown Grant was issued to Park in July 1866. But the 'single tree' was a noted geographical feature which could be seen from many miles away and was sometimes known as the 'tapu tree'. Tradition has it that the large matai (black pine) was a survivor of the ancient rain-forest podocarps of the Canterbury Plains and for generations stood proud of the surrounding bush. The 1,000 year old tree beckoned in the autumn season to Maori who would come from as far afield as Banks Peninsula and Kaiapoi, to trap rats and to gather and dry the ripe berries – which the pigeons and other birds they caught there had grown fat upon. The tree was called the tree of Hine Paaka. Hine Paaka was a wife of the 17th century Ngai Tahu chief Maru. (Curiously the name 'Paaka' is a transliteration of the English name Park to Maori.) By the time of Park's 1862 surveys, the surrounding bush had been felled but the old tree served as a reference point for the surveyor.

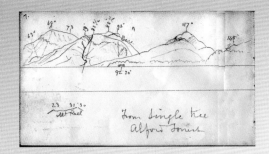

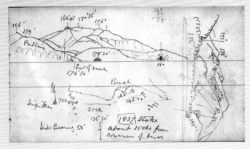

A field book sketch showing the 'Tapu Tree' used as a reference point.

R Park FB 177 OS LINZ Christchurch.

A photo of the original 'Tapu Tree, Hine Paaka'.

19XX.2.543 Canterbury Museum.

The memorial on Highway 77 near Alford Forest. The plaque tells of Hine Paaka being a sapling when Maori came to Aotearoa – New Zealand. The 'fowling tree' by 1930 was a dead skeleton, and on 30 September 1945, a gale finally toppled the ancient matai. A piece of this tree is in the Ashburton Museum. The famous 'Single Tree' has now been replaced with a new sapling planted in September 1976 'To symbolise the Unity' of Maori and Pakeha. Now the sapling matai grows high above the stone wall.

Photos Frank Easdale.

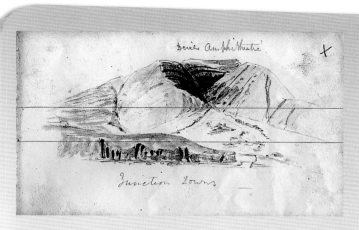

Three of several pages of sketches made by Robert Park in 1862 in his field books. Sometimes station cottages are depicted in these but are often unnamed.

FB 177 OS LINZ Christchurch.

from some numbness, a few severe scratches and the total destruction of his clothing, Browning was as right as rain. Greenlaw, however, noted that when they got home at 5 p.m. he found his boots frozen to his two pairs of socks, and ice had formed between his toes. The incident caused them to alter the route at this point a couple of days later when, despite having to constantly shovel snow, they got a good deal higher. The 31st saw sleet and snow, thunder and lightning, and the day was spent in their blankets, 'no tea nor nothing', moaned Newberry.

August, and more snow, but they rigged a shanty to cook in. That night letters came from Christchurch and it was learned that poor Trounce had died. Jenkins was so cut up that he would later 'give £100, a large sum', to the widow and children. The men were understandably upset and it seems a proposal about this time to reduce their daily rates stirred one hand Jim to use 'the following language' to Greenlaw who duly reported it to Mr. Park. 'If the other men would hold you I would sew up your arse for you or any other Buggers who would reduce their pay to 8/- pr. day.' What the outcome was is not said!

At length on the 4th a hut was building. Park drew a view of the place this day. Five packhorses with stores came on the day Newberry was chaining down the creek with Browning, when he slipped in, getting wet through. His clothes froze solid in the 200 yards back to camp. Greenlaw (they had nicknamed him Greenhorn) went with Park to look at the Pass. Three more packhorses turned up with sheep from Glenthorne Station. Sunday was marked with a dinner of roast beef and currant pudding, with Park serving out a glass of grog to all hands. Two days later the hut 26 x 13 feet with two rooms, one with eight bunks and one for eating was finished, with a double tarpaulin roof over the rafters, and a fire lit in it for the first time. The stone and clay chimney drew well.

The next morning – a hard frost but a beautiful day – Park, Browning and Newberry 'went and got on to the top of the Pass, it took one hour and twenty minutes' to get up the steep face of 1,500 feet, with snow so deep in places it looked blue. They were at the top for three hours looking at 'the proposed direct road' onto Hokitika. Park would not go on with the survey from here – that was left to John Browning, but on the day they parted company, Park's party went with the others to the summit, where they took a rest and had 'a tot of grog all round from a bottle brought up on purpose, and which was thrown far and high over the cliff with three cheers', recorded Money. According to Greenlaw, Robert Park came down from the top in 17 minutes, 'rather face down & sliding most of the way'. The next day he was on his way home to Winchmore.

Park's report on the West Coast Road by the North Rakaia route, was dated 28 August at Winchmore, and presented to the Canterbury Provincial Council together with the plans drawn by Park shown here. He optimistically wrote that there would be little difficulty in cutting a track for stock at a fair gradient and that 'should the Government determine to eventually form a dray road that can also be accomplished at not a very great cost'. The dray road never happened. That would go by way of Arthur Dobson's route over Arthur's Pass.

The Grey Mare's Tail. A painting by Robert Park of the waterfall up to the south-west from the beginning of the zig-zag to the glacier.

Courtesy Heather Murchison.

Park's name was memorialised in the naming of Mount Park as seen on the original 1865 plan. But as my surveyor husband found, after poring over maps and documents the name has had some four successive locations, each a higher peak, in reaching its present location on the Whitcombe 1:50,000 map, J34. The original point named was likely no more than a convenient knoll above the valley floor on the bend of the Wilberforce River which Park and Browning flagged as a control point, the 'Mount', given the alpine setting, being somewhat tongue-in-cheek. On a later 1884 topographical plan Mount Park has been promoted some 2.4 kilometres up the Eliot Ridge to an elevation of about 1,890 metres. A further plan in 1906 has moved the location another 2.4 kilometres on to the Main Divide at an elevation of 1,954 metres, and now it graces a peak 1.3 kilometres south-west of Mount Eliot with an elevation of 2,036 metres, in association with various 'Mungo' named features. It is doubtful the present Mount Park can be seen from any point where Park and Browning might have seen it and quite certain that Robert Park never climbed the presently named peak.

It is as well to clear up misconceptions, too, about the names 'Mungo River', 'Mungo Pass', and 'Mungo Peak'. It has been thought by Park descendants that Robert Park gave the names in surveys he did here, to perpetuate the name of his imagined illustrious relative. Not so. Nobody surveyed in the Mungo valley area until well into the 1890s and Park was dead in 1870. Gold prospectors ventured in, in the 1880s, but on the maps is a large blank space in that area. It is not until 1906 with a geological survey that the Mungo names are first recorded. I have not found who first named these features, but it seems likely they were first so named in association with Mount Park. Mungo Park was still, in the late 19th century, a Boy's Own hero to be found in great tales of exploration.

Mention has been made of Glenthorne, Major Scott's station near the Wilberforce/Harper confluence, where the wounded Trounce was taken and where sheep were supplied for feeding the men in Park's and Browning's party. Park put in his diary after staying overnight (probably 1862/3) at Glenthorne, 'very cold I found it'. Glenthorne Station along with Lake Coleridge, Oakden and Acheron Bank Stations would later be part of many thousands of acres in the Murchison family's hands. Molly Park, a granddaughter of Robert Park's from this third family would become Ken Murchison's wife and live at Lake Coleridge and Glenthorne.

Park was back farming at Winchmore in 1868 when a telegram came at the beginning of January from his old friend Donald McLean. Could he come up to Napier to value some of McLean's holdings? Park replied, 'Your pay is so good that I cannot resist the offer & so will leave immediately for Napier although we will begin shearing in a couple of days, but as I have a good man as overseer (a Highlander!) it does not so much signify'. This 'good man' was probably Duncan Cameron. He might bring Mrs Park with him, who had never been to Napier. He is 'so glad to hear that Mary is better'. His daughter Mary, from his first family, has now been married to John Kinross for above six years, and seems to have been up and down with illness as hints in some of Donald McLean's sisters' letters tell.

Top right: 'The Wreck of the *Echunga*'. Loaded with wool and hides the *Echunga* dragged her anchor in the Napier roadstead, and broke her back when driven ashore on 3 February 1868.

R Park. Courtesy David Deans Estate.

Right: The *Echunga* foundering in February 1868. This scene, carefully trimmed may have been intended by Edith Park for her scrapbook. The scene could serve as a reminder of stories told of her half-sisters' experience of the wreck of the *Sobraon* twenty years earlier.

R Park. Courtesy David Deans Estate.

Knross — Alloway Park

Mount Alloway, the home on Bluff Hill, Napier of Robert Mary Anne's daughter Mary Jane who married John Kinross. Robert Park visited here, possibly with Mary Jane's stepmother Marion, in 1868. It would be the last time Robert would see his eldest child.

R Park 1972.123.17 Canterbury Museum.

Imperial Troops' quarters at Napier, 1868. A safeguard against a feared Hauhau uprising.

R Park 1970.123.3 Canterbury Museum.

167

A painting of Onepoto Gully on Scinde Island (Bluff Hill) Napier where Donald McLean had a property in 1868.

R Park 1969.122.11 Canterbury Museum

Park hadn't been back to Hawkes Bay since March 1861 (before Mary was married in September) when he had been surveying for McLean at his station at Maraekakaho which was being added to incrementally. Whether Marion Park went with him to Napier in 1868 is uncertain. She certainly visited Kate Hart (Robert Hart and Kate McLean, Donald McLean's sister had been married in 1867) in Wellington, who gave her a large luncheon party and this was in January (the year not given). Kate thought that Marion had enjoyed her visit to Wellington, though she says Marion has not got to Napier where her son George was then. Did he go with his father? Kate was expecting another visit from Mrs Park and her girls, so presumably it was summer holidays, and Edith and Minnie had also come to Wellington from Winchmore.

She asks brother Donald in Hawkes Bay to give her love to dear Mrs Kinross. Mary Kinross evidently came to Wellington on occasion as at one time Kate writes of going up to Napier by steamer with Mrs Kinross.

Robert Park may have been to Wellington at times from Winchmore. Jane Deans writes of returning from Wellington to Christchurch, when, seasick as usual, she is grateful that her 13-year-old John is sharing a cabin with Robert. Robert's son George was 13 also and also at High School in Christchurch. And his daughters Edith and Minnie he no doubt would see

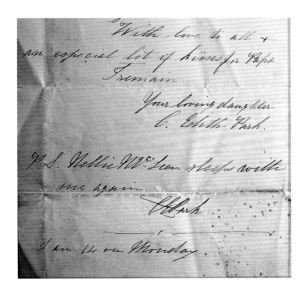

Almost-14-year-old Catherine Edith Park's letter to her 'darling Mamma' Marion at Winchmore, from Mrs Thomson's school, Avon House in Christchurch.
Deans Family Papers, Riccarton Bush Trust.

at Mrs Thomson's school when passing through Christchurch.

On 19 February 1870, Marion and Robert's elder daughter is writing to her 'darling Mamma' from Avon House, Mrs Thomson's famous school. She was glad to get her mother's letter, for 'Thursday is like an Oasis in the Sahara. I mean that I am very happy at school but that it is so pleasant to hear from you … Pia has sent our petticoats and my skirt it is trimmed up the front with black velvet bows. Georgie sent me a very pretty Valentine'. She wants Mamma to send a letter to Minnie 'full of scolding'. She, Minnie, has put on Edith's new house boots and got them covered with dust 'and it is no good my talking to her'. Mrs Thomson had taken them yesterday to the school feast – 700 children 'on the ground' from St Michael's, St Luke's, St John's and Teddington.

She has heard from Mrs Thomson of her Papa's illness, and so finishes her letter, 'With love to all & an especial lot of kisses for Papa.

I remain
Your loving daughter
C. Edith Park.

P.S. Nellie McLean sleeps with me again.
C.E.Park.
I am 14 on Monday.'

Robert Park never recovered from his illness said to be 'inflammation of the lungs' and died at Cranmer Square in Christchurch on Thursday 10 March 1870. He had turned 58 in January. He was buried at Addington Cemetry on the Sunday.

Robert Park's name is perpetuated in the names of streets in Wellington, Wanganui, Dunedin and Ashburton, of Park Island at Napier, and of Mount Park in the Southern Alps.

Marion Park – the 'darling Mamma'.
Courtesy Heather Murchison.

Photos of the ageing, snowy-bearded Robert Park taken in Wellington in Wigglesworth's Studio, most likely in 1868.

Courtesy Heather Murchison.

Had a fond daughter embroidered the papa's smoking cap?

Courtesy Heather Murchison.

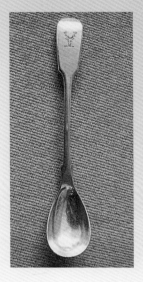

A drawing of the Park badge.

Frank Easdale.

Above: Photos of a small spoon with the Park crest badge emblem engraved on it. The whole crest badge is also shown on a photo of the seal. There is one complete example of this seal on an envelope of a letter sent to Donald McLean from Wanganui, 24 October 1852, in the McLean Papers MS 0032 A.T.L.

The crest badge is the one which Park is wearing on his bonnet on page 200. The crest motto is 'I commit myself to providence'.

The buck's head is derived from a Park coat of arms which sports three bucks' heads on a gold shield with a chequered band in silver and blue which apparently originated with a Park of Fulfordlees (1672-7) on the east coast of the Borders.

Photos of these items courtesy of Robin Park who was the Robin whom cousin May Cumbrae-Stewart from Melbourne, in 1931, would take for walks. (See p 64 Chapter 13.)

MONTROSE & RICCARTON HOUSE – FAMILIES ENTWINED

With Robert Park's untimely death at 58, the focus of this story changes from one man, to his three families, his first, second and third, his children and a few of his grandchildren. This exploration will lead to four gathering places of the families, and to Mungo Park's trunk and its Kaitiaki.

After his shift to Winchmore, Robert Park had made a will in September 1862. In this he had provided for the two daughters of his first family (by Mary Anne) Mary Jane and Agnes, leaving them Park Cottage on The Terrace in Wellington. (The area here had been re-

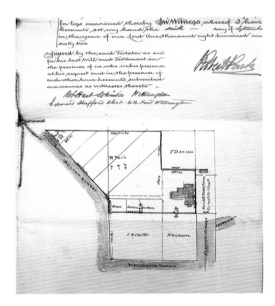

A sketch of the 'footprint' from Robert Park's will of Park Cottage in Kumutoto Street left to the two daughters of his first family, Mary Jane Kinross and Agnes Stewart.

CH 171A713/1870 Archives New Zealand/ Te Rua Mahara o te Kawanatanga Christchurch Regional Office.

Catherine Edith and Elizabeth Marion when they lived in Wellington with their widowed mother Marion.

Courtesy Heather Murchison.

duced by 5 perches bought for a sexton's cottage for the Bolton Street Cemetery in 1857.) The Park property was to be sold, or rented until sold, the money realised to be invested and the income from this to be paid the girls. Marion Park was to inherit the rest of his estate, the proceeds from the sale of any properties to be invested at her will in a residence 'or in sheep or cattle'. There is no mention of his second family by Terenui.

Marion didn't stay on very long at Winchmore, perhaps a year? There was a sad memory associated with Winchmore. Captain John McLean of the Buccleugh run was thrown from his overturned buggy and died, when turning into the Winchmore gateway in 1871. His family had fallen on hard times, had been obliged to give up Buccleugh and were living at Winchmore thanks to George Hart's generosity and the close family associations. McLean's ghost is said to hover by the gate.

Sadder too, in that year Mary Jane Kinross, the eldest daughter of Robert and Mary Anne, had died in Wellington on 23 October 1871 of a wasting disease. She was only 29, and had been a shadowy figure in Napier, with indifferent health for some years. The marriage had not been blessed with children. Across the Tasman, however, Mary's sister Agnes, of the first family had, on 10 August, at St Kilda, Melbourne, Victoria, given birth to a daughter, after three sons. This child, Mary Isobel Stewart, would have special associations with her New Zealand cousins at Riccarton House.

Robert Hart's wife, Donald McLean's sister Catherine (Kate), is writing to her sister Annabella in Napier in 1870. Kate had been away from their Wellington home in Hobson Street to where she had hurried back on getting a telegram from Robert saying he was 'laid up'. But, on her return she wrote that though she had 'found him getting about the truth is, that he feels Mr Park's death and from what I heard the burden of the widow and family will to a large extent fall upon him'. Park was in debt when he died, she says, 'and Mrs Park having parted with some of her (inheritance?) is coming to live in Wellington' and will stay with them for a time. Kate is rather put out by all this disturbance, and longs for her sister, Annabella, to confide in as she has no one, for 'Robert is too much taken with his own family'. Hardly surprising at this time. Robert Hart was after all Marion's brother and her solicitor, and their brother George Hart, along with John Kinross (Mary Jane's husband in Napier) were trustees together with Marion, of Park's estate. The situation was probably not as bleak as Kate had described. There were assets in land, such as the 50 acres at Heathcote in Christchurch, 20 acres at Alford Forest and possibly some town sections in Ashburton. Whether he still had the Wanganui property is doubtful. The Hon. George Buckley of Casterton in the Heathcote Valley was to receive title to the 50-acre Park property near his, in January 1876. Although Marion Park notes in 1879 that the Buckleys had sold Casterton and were moving to Wellington, the 50-acre block was not registered to the new owner until 1885. An inventory of his assets which Park desired to be made has not been found but probate was given in May 1870, just two months after his death.

How long Marion and her family stayed with her brother and his wife in Hobson Street is not known, but by 1875 and probably earlier she was in Hawkestone Street in Wellington, either owning or renting a house there. Young Robert George, called George, who had been living with Uncle Robert Hart when his father died, had been successful in passing the Junior and Senior Civil Service exams in one year, 1872. The bright lad was sports minded too, and was one of the founders of the Wellington Football Club. He would represent Wellington Province as half-back. His career in surveying and engineering began with his appointment as a cadet on the Rimutaka railway. The middle of 1878 found him with a team of eight men surveying a railway route from the Hutt Valley to Pauatahanui and on to the Kapiti Coast. An undertaking, Uncle Robert Hart writes, which would be just as difficult as the Rimutaka line. Shades of George's father Robert and the Bristol/Exeter line, though the latter would have been over much gentler terrain. Robert Park had no doubt speculated in his journeyings over from Porirua and along the Kapiti Coast on how a railway line here might one day be engineered. Now speculation was to become reality.

At the beginning of that year, 1878, George had been at the wedding of his sister Elizabeth Marion Park (Minnie). She was wed to the man she intended while still at school to marry, Dr William Henry Symes, M.D., R.N. of Christchurch, at St Paul's Church in Wellington on 21 February. This (pro-Cathedral) in Mulgrave Street was new, not the old St. Paul's where her half-sister

Edith and Minnie's brother George in his heyday.

Courtesy David Deans Estate.

Mary Jane had married John Kinross in 1861. The new church, a lovely building, is now called 'Old St Pauls'. Minnie would go to live in Christchurch. From Uncle Robert comes a sharp comment in May, that 'Mrs Symes has not sent us directly or indirectly a word of acknowledgement of a wedding gift'. Robert and wife Kate, from extant letters, seem given to acerbic remarks about their young female relatives and the in-laws. Robert Hart's surviving letters were mostly to young Douglas Maclean, Kate McLean's nephew, who was overseas. Douglas was a year older than Robert's other nephew George Park, both of whom found favour with him; the uncle who stood as parent to the fatherless young men. Robert Park's old friend 'Mac', then Sir Donald McLean, had died in January 1877, but Douglas had long been in the care of Sir Donald's sisters, his aunts Kate and Annabella. Annabella still lived at Maraekakaho on the McLean farm.

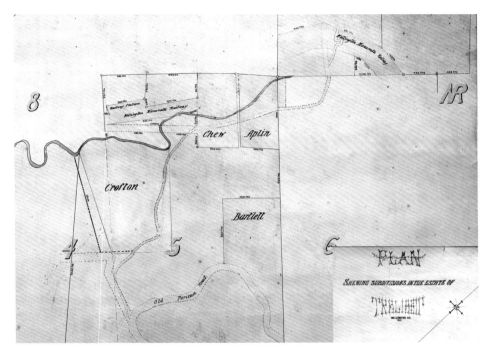

Details from a plan of a subdivision of Captain Daniell's farm Trelissic surveyed by Robert Park's son George, which is dated 1881. It shows the old Kaiwharawhara road from Wellington to Porirua which Robert Park walked and rode along many a time from the earliest years of Wellington. The Wellington – Manawatu rail also goes partly through the estate. George was in a party which surveyed a line beyond Porirua to the Kapiti Coast.

Map Coll. 832 4799gbbd/Ng/1881 A.T.L.

Robert and Kate Hart paid a visit to the South Island in September 1878 staying with Captain McLean's widow. The Parks, that is Mrs and Edith, had also been south from Wellington to see Minnie Symes. Edith returned to Wellington engaged to John Deans of Riccarton. 'Two more unfortunates you will say' wrote Uncle Robert to Douglas. Marion Park was back in Christchurch in the middle of December 1878 to be with a very pregnant Minnie. On 10 January 1879 she presented Marion with a little grandson.

Edith had been staying with Minnie for most of October until Marion arrived. No doubt during this time, and until the end of February when they both returned to Wellington, Edith had been seeing quite a lot of her betrothed, John Deans II, paying numerous visits to Riccarton House and her future mother-in-law Jane Deans. It had been intended to bring Minnie back to Wellington, and they had all boarded the steamer at Lyttelton, when they were dismayed to find it was so crowded the stewardesses could not give Minnie with her six-week-old baby a berth. Marion sent her home, as she felt the young mother was not strong enough to stand the trip without a cabin.

Edith's marriage was set for June 1879 and a month before the wedding Minnie and baby finally joined them at Marion Park's house in Molesworth Street. Minnie was looking thin 'but baby was a fine healthy boy' wrote Marion Park. Minnie and baby

The lovely Minnie Park who married Dr William Henry Symes in Wellington on 21 February 1878.

Courtesy Heather Murchison.

Langford Park Symes were with them for six weeks and would go home to Christchurch much stronger. It was quite a business preparing a trousseau for Edith but they'd found an excellent local woman, Mrs Paul. Ah, but the wedding dress. As with Minnie's gown, Marion Park sent to Agnes Stewart (her stepdaughter) in Melbourne for material. This time though, at Agnes' suggestion, it was also made there and delivered to Wellington a week before the wedding. The gown of white satin trimmed with lace and flowers fitted perfectly. Minnie made her a wreath of orange blossom, jasmine and myrtle, and over all went a tulle veil, and round her neck a present from the bridegroom, a gold necklet and diamond locket. She had five bridesmaids the principal one being 'Miss McLean from Auckland'. (She was a daughter of Benjamin McLean who was a tenant farmer at St Johns College, but not a relative of Robert Hart's wife Kate.) The chief bridesmaid

A photo of William Symes taken in Edinburgh. The man Minnie was so set on marrying when a school girl.

Courtesy Michael Symes.

was in white cashmere and ruby satin, Fanny and Sarah Brandon in pink Japanese silk, and the two young cousins, Lily and Minnie Hart echoing Miss McLean in white and ruby. All wore silk caps, and gold lockets, gifts from John Deans. The ceremony was in the new Scotch church, not quite finished, St Andrews, on The Terrace. George Hart (the owner of several southern sheep runs) and his family, wife Julia, sons Robbie and Reg, Lily and Minnie and infant son were up from Canterbury, and were staying with Robert and Kate Hart. (George had been returned to Parliament earlier as member for the Lake Coleridge district but was to lose the seat later that year.)

Twenty-four sat down to the wedding feast, all relatives or connections of the bride and groom, except for the minister, Mr Ogg, who had taken the 'solemn and earnest' service. Was a relative from the old country at the reception? In May, Robert Hart had had to dinner, a Mr and Mrs Harrison. Mrs Harrison, on a visit to New Zealand, was the former widow of Robert Park's famous Scottish sculptor brother, Patric. One might suppose them at the wedding of Robina Harrison's niece.

Robert Hart wrote of the events of July to Douglas Maclean. The wedding, he said, had gone off smoothly but he hoped that when his nephew George Park took the plunge it might be in the company of one worthy of him. George had had 'very hard and rough Railway surveying'. Did George stand in for his late father in giving the bride away? He certainly was a witness, signing the register, his address being given as Public Works, Featherston. He must have been back surveying on the extension of the Rimutaka railway line as it was being pushed through to Masterton. The young couple, Edith and John, took a trip to Featherston by railway following their marriage, the fell engines fore and aft pushing and pulling the carriages on the Rimutaka incline over the steep-sided mountain range to the Wairarapa.

John and Edith dined with Uncle Robert and Aunt Kate when they returned after a couple of days and were just leaving when the fire bells were heard ringing. The Opera House in Manners Street was burning, and as John and Edith were lodging at the nearby Albert Hotel they stayed the night at Hawkestone Street with the Harts. The next day they were off south to Christchurch – and Edith's new life at Riccarton House.

Minnie Symes and baby Langford left Marion Park's a fortnight later, but kind Miss McLean, the chief bridesmaid,

Catherine Edith in Wellington before her wedding to John Deans with sister Minnie (Symes) on the left, and Uncle George Hart's daughters Minnie and Lily, who would be her bridesmaids.

Courtesy Heather Murchison.

kept Marion company for a little longer before going back to Auckland. Marion misses Edith very much She was so good at organising, she wrote to Annabella McLean, but she shouldn't grumble, as she was lucky Edith had stayed with her so long. Just now she could wish for her help as she was altering the room arrangements. She has leased her Molesworth Street home to a Mrs [Donaghue?] who will board her. This means

180

Catherine Edith Park and John Deans II just before their marriage in June 1879 at the new Scotch Church, St Andrews on The Terrace, Wellington.

Courtesy Heather Murchison.

she would be free to come and go as she pleases, no doubt anticipating visits to both daughters in Christchurch.

Her son George transferred to the Patea – Normanby railway in south Taranaki, and then, leaving railway employ from 1880, he worked for the Waikato Road Board. It is possible his mother was with him for a time. Robert and Kate Hart had come back to Wellington from a visit to Sydney (via Christchurch as was usual) in February 1880 to find Marion Park and son George in town, both looking well. In January Marion had had Minnie with her once more and had been to the Lady Mayoress's picnic which 200 attended at Homewood, Karori, with Robert Hart. Kate Hart had been too ill with rheumatism to go and although Marion and daughter Minnie were equal to going up and down the hill, Robert was not and stayed with the 'mature ladies and got a very good lunch'.

The Harts did not get to Melbourne on their Australian visit. If they had they would have found Agnes Stewart and her husband and the first family cousins comfortably settled in their new home, Montrose, at Brighton Beach. Agnes and Francis Stewart had seven children at this time: Francis, Edward (Ted), Charles, Mary Isobell (May), Gordon Kinross (Tom), Frederick, and the infant Beatrice Emily Bannatyne born on 10 November 1879. Two more surviving children were to be born at Montrose, Reginald in 1881 and Janet in 1883.

Catherine Edith's wedding dress was originally of white satin trimmed with lace and flowers. At a later date, ruby satin ruched and pleated, transformed the bridal gown to one to be worn in the evening. *1961.89.1 Canterbury Museum.*

Edith would equal her half-sister Agnes in, as Gordon Ogilvie puts it in *Pioneers of the Plains*, *The Deans of Riccarton*, 'admirable fertility'. The first of Edith and John's children, John Deans III, had been born on 7 June 1880 and Uncle Robert Hart informs Douglas Maclean that 'There have been rejoicings at a Christening at Riccarton House of a son and heir'. Marion Park did get to see stepdaughter Agnes in January of 1881 when she went to Melbourne, again leaving from Christchurch where she would have seen the six-month-old Deans grandson, and also Minnie's second child. There is no written record of Marion Park's stay at Montrose with Agnes and her seven nieces and nephews, ranging from Bea at three to Francis at 16, but a few photos which the George

Riccarton House ca 1890. Edith Park came here as a bride in 1879, five years after the house had been substantially enlarged: anticipating the many children? The front portion remains with a dormer window and a bay window added and the verandah partly enclosed.

Deans Family Papers, Riccarton Bush Trust.

Park descendants have could date from that time. She was happy to meet an old friend of her London youth, Dr Tweedale, who was in practice in Melbourne.

In January, Marion's brother Robert Hart is writing his weekly letter to nephew Douglas Maclean. He has indigestion which makes him costive in expression he says. Douglas shouldn't take all he writes too seriously as 'the simple lines written are for my own and your amusement'. He continues, 'Depend upon it I would not like to see you resemble the Laird of Riccarton. He is all very well in his way but to speak the truth is not by temperament or training fitted to perform the duties of a man of his property and stake in the country'. But the 'Laird' had a wise mother in Jane Deans and capable

Likenesses of Edith and John Deans taken in Edinburgh on their trip to Europe in 1881. They left baby John III (Ian) to be cared for by his 'two grandmas'.

Courtesy Heather Murchison.

uncles to help and advise him; Douglas had Uncle Robert, and his message of 'property has its duties' and his loving aunts as his advisors. Uncle Robert a week or so later writes Douglas in England, 'The Squire of Riccarton and his wife are going to England leaving the heir in charge of his two grandmas. I am heartily glad of this he is to my mind one who may under wise guidance be made a good deal of but who's training hitherto has been altogether too [naïve?] for the position which his wealth makes it a duty upon him to assume. From what I saw of him at the wedding I believe him to be possessed of very good qualities If he should make you out you may be of use to him.' (Whether Douglas Maclean and John Deans II met in Britain is not known.)

In July 1881 Edith and John Deans left for Melbourne on their way to Europe. Surely they visited Edith's Aunt Agnes at Montrose, but again there is no account of this. Accompanying them were Mr and Mrs Wilkins, whose family would later be joined to that of Park descendants. 'The Deanses have left their son and heir a sturdy youngster (who) upon his seat on the Hearth looks round with an air as satisfied as if he were already in possession – Absit omen', writes Robert Hart. In July Robert has just seen his nephew George Park for the first time for many months. George has been over to the West Coast by rail and coach on a mission for Uncle George Hart. 'He describes the scenery as beautiful and Grand in the extreme.' This was the route over Arthurs Pass, the route favoured for a coach road and then railway, north of the Brownings Pass route surveyed by Park and Browning sixteen years before.

No doubt Agnes Stewart used this visiting-card case when making new aquaintances in Melbourne. It is now cherished by a great-granddaughter, Gillian Webster.

Photo courtesy Stewart Robinson.

The litany desk which was in St Peter's, St Kilda, Melbourne. This desk was carved by Beatrice Cumbrae-Stewart, daughter of Agnes Stewart (née Park). The desk has the initials of six of the family on it. It is now in the Brighton Museum.

Courtesy Stewart Robinson.

E.C.WADDINGTON & CO.

E.C.WADDINGTON & CO.

Far left: Beatrice Emily Bannatyne Stewart. Bea was given the name Bannatyne for Agnes' Aunt Bannatyne, the former Emily Jane Morgan, sister of Mary Anne Park, and widow of Major Baker.

Courtesy Heather Murchison

Left: Young Fred Stewart.

Courtesy Heather Murchison.

E.C.WADDINGTON & CO.

Far left: Probably Mary Isobel (May) Stewart the eldest girl with some brothers?

Courtesy Heather Murchison.

Left: The three Stewart daughters in Sunday best. May is seated, Bea is on her right and, in the black shoes, is the youngest child Janet.

Courtesy Heather Murchison.

Francis Edward Stewart, the fashionably bearded husband of Agnes.

Courtesy June Cumbrae-Stewart

Elegant Agnes Stewart (née Park). A photograph taken in Melbourne after the Stewarts had moved there.

Courtesy Gillian Webster

At Montrose, St Kilda, Melbourne.

The lower drawing room.

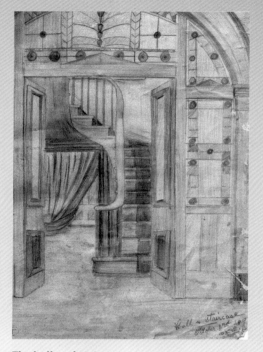

The hall and staircase.

Sketches by Beatrice Cumbrae-Stewart. Courtesy Stewart Robinson.

The 'small buggy' – one of three at Montrose, drawn by May Cumbrae-Stewart.

Courtesy Stewart Robinson.

The Stewart family in front of Montrose as family who visited from New Zealand would have seen their home.

Courtesy Gillian Webster.

Brighton Beach, near Montrose, looking north (Jones Point) Melbourne 1896. Painted by May Cumbrae-Stewart.

Courtesy Stewart Robinson.

The Wilderness, The Stewarts' holiday retreat.

Painted by Beatrice Cumbrae-Stewart.
Courtesy Stewart Robinson.

George and Mary Ferguson
Park. They married in 1886 in
Southbridge, Canterbury.

Courtesy Heather Murchison.

January 1882, and Marion Park is dining at her brother Robert Hart's in Wellington along with their brother George Hart and four of his children. Quite a family party notes Robert, and they sit in the sun in the afternoon. Perhaps it is not often the two ageing Hart brothers and their sister get together? I think Marion's son George must have been there too. He was to leave that week for Southbridge 'to take up the business with the proprietorship of the newspaper published there', the *Ellesmere Guardian*. A railway branch line ran from Christchurch to Southbridge. He would be here six years, so he couldn't have got the job he'd applied for in August of that year as an architect in the North Canterbury Education District. In Southbridge he was to meet and marry Mary Campbell Ferguson, the second daughter of Robert (a deceased schoolmaster) and Elizabeth Ferguson, on 3 February 1886. In December 1886 a son Robert was born to the couple.

Mother Marion Park had no children in Wellington now, but apparently had no inclination to go back to the South Island to live. However, in 1882 Marion had her hands full for a fortnight, nursing a son (William Napier Park?) of Patric Park, who was in New Zealand working as an engineer at the Petone Railway Workshops (established in1876). Robert Hart says he 'was smitten with a sunstroke at Parihaka and this no doubt with solitary living has led to a brain fever'. It's a puzzle why he should have been at Parihaka, Te Whiti's village there having been destroyed in late 1881. Whether young George and his cousin from Britain came across each other in the couple of years he was living in Petone is unknown.

There was always much family to-ing and fro-ing between Wellington and the South Island. In November 1883 the Robert Harts were in Canterbury staying with Mrs. McLean and seeing a good deal of Nellie McLean (who had been at Mrs Thomson's school with Edith and Minnie) of whom they were very fond. On this trip they visited Riccarton House and the Deans farm at Homebush. The latter made a great impression, as Robert was always taken with scientific and technical advances; and here water power was used for all the

THE NEW ZEALAND, PHOTOGRAPHIC COY. WELLINGTON.

An older Marion Park in Wellington.
Courtesy Heather Murchison.

work at the farm and home to which it could be made applicable; a hydraulic ram kept the cisterns full and automatically supplied constant fresh water. We don't hear anything of grandnieces or grandnephews. But by the end of 1883 a daughter had been added to John and Edith's family named Marion for her maternal grandmother.

In 1883 also, Agnes and Francis Stewart's last surviving child was born, Janet, in December at Montrose in Melbourne. That family was growing up. Francis Stewart was 20 when this sister was born, and would soon be on his way to Christchurch, Oxford, where he took second-class honours in modern history, and in 1887 was called to the

Bar at the Inner Temple. 1888 saw him back in Melbourne where he practiced as a solicitor.

There was no mention by the Harts on their trip south of visiting nephew George at Southbridge. George Park had, however, settled comfortably into life there. By 1886 a note appeared in the *Lyttelton Times*. R.G.Park, the indefatigable Secretary of the Caledonian Society, 'was the recipient of a handsome gold medal and a purse of sovereigns'. It had been a jolly evening with all nationalities present, but the happy, all 'Scotch' contingent walking home mistook gorse for heather and ended up very much scratched. Almost two years later in September 1888 a 'Valedictory' appeared in the *Lyttelton Times*. George Park was being farewelled

Prof. Francis William Sutton Cumbrae- Stewart, sometime Garrick Professor of Law at Brisbane University.

Courtesy Stewart Robinson.

at the Royal Hotel Southbridge as he was leaving the district where he had always taken an active part to 'advance the welfare of the township. In athletic circles he would be greatly missed, for he was an enthusiast, and possessed the secret of instilling enthusiasm in others'. He hadn't made a fortune in the district but 'money could not purchase the esteem and respect in which he was held'. A toast was drunk with 'musical honours', eliciting a 'feeling response' from George. Not a word was said about his reason for leaving.

As a newspaper proprietor he had not done well in Southbridge. After four years he was filing for bankruptcy, unable to pay wages or rent. His main creditors, however, were his mother Marion and his uncle George Hart and one other. A month after filing (on the advice of his solicitor – Uncle Robert Hart) he had agreed that his mother should have his survey instruments and furniture conveyed to her in lieu of payment. He would be forgiven some debts, and by April 1889 the wages claim was cleared and in June that year he gained his discharge from bankruptcy. Of course those survey instruments were with George when he perforce took up railway surveying once more. He and wife Mary

George and Mary Park's three children Robert, Molly and Reggie about the turn of the century. Mary had died in 1896.

Courtesy Heather Murchison.

had moved to Reefton, the South Island West Coast gold town on the Inangahua River where their next child, Mary Roberta (Molly), was born. Incidentally Reefton was the first town in New Zealand to have hydro-electric power in 1888, a facility which Mary Park might have appreciated. George was often away from home and Mary's health was not good. Rainy Reefton would not have helped. The family then moved to the kinder climate of Blenheim where George practiced as an architect and civil engineer, being also for four years an overseer to the Awatere Road Board which controlled a good deal of the Marlborough district. In Blenheim in October 1893 George Reginald was born. Then tragedy. Three years later, in September 1896, a son, John, was born who died after three days. A month after the birth the mother, Mary, also died. George heroically looked after his three children for nine years by which time they were 19, 16 and 12. Then he too died at only 52 years of age in 1905.

George Park in his will had named his nephew John Deans III (Ian of Homebush, the 'heir' born to Edith and John Deans II in 1880) and George's sister Edith Deans

Molly Park, who went to live at Riccarton House with her Aunt Edith Deans following her father's death in 1905. She was married from here in 1913. Molly is on the right in this photo taken in 1910 in front of Riccarton House.

Deans Family Papers, Riccarton Bush Trust.

(née Park) Ian Dean's mother and his children's aunt, as guardians. Molly went immediately to live at Riccarton House, while, George Reginald (Reggie) was to follow by 1907 when he was at Christchurch Boys High School. Reggie spent much holiday time at his much older cousin and guardian Ian's farm at Homebush and saw his sister Molly at Riccarton House on occasion.

When Molly went to Riccarton House in 1905 her Aunt Edith's eight living children would have ranged in age from John III, (Ian) at 25 to Stuart Maxwell, around about eight. Edith's husband John II had died in 1902. His mother Jane Deans was still the matriarch of Riccarton House and would outlive her only son by nine years. She died in 1911, two years before Molly Park was married from Riccarton House to Ken Murchison of Lake Coleridge Station in 1913.

There had been an anxious letter from Molly's older brother, another Robert Park, who by this time had gone to Australia and was living in Sydney. Writing in February 1912 he tells Ken that Molly had borne the brunt of her father's illness when 'the play time of life became to her a long vigil'. She should now have 'all the happiness that she could get'. As Ken has a close friendship with Ian Deans, the latter's judgment he feels he can rely on, even more than Aunt Edith's as he believes in a man's judgment more than that of a woman. Although Ken is a stranger to him, they and others think he is

Glenthorne on the Wilberforce in winter, where Molly and Ken Murchison first lived for a short time. In 1865, Glenthorne station and the homestead belonged to Major Scott and the party of men employed on the Brownings Pass survey would have mutton meals made with the sheep from these hills. Molly and Ken came back to Glenthorne in 1931 for eight years.

Courtesy Catherine McQueen.

the right man to make up for the loss of, first her mother, then her father. And as for Ken, he has 'really got a prize'. He also informs Ken that Molly who has told him she and Ken are to be 'dreadfully poor' is to come into her inheritance in about three years. The money will be held by the trustees (Ian Deans and himself) and the income paid to Molly. She had been left two thirds of George's estate, the other third having been divided earlier between his three children. Robert trusts that their 'future life will fall in pleasant places', wishes him the best of luck, and exhorts him, 'be good to my only sister'. (Robert was to die at Paschendale in 1917, his younger brother Reggie, though wounded, would survive that battle.)

Molly and Ken made their first home at the cottage on the Glenthorne run (where in 1865 her grandfather Robert had been when surveying Brownings Pass), then in 1914, when Ken's mother died, moved to the Lake Coleridge cottage on the Lake Coleridge run. Then into the Lake Coleridge homestead, where their son Bobs Murchison was born in 1916. Later, they farmed in the Kirwee district for some years. In 1931 they returned to Glenthorne, their first home, where they stayed until 1939 and then made a shift to Christchurch City. In the 1930's, Agnes' eldest daughter, over from Australia, had stayed at Glenthorne. This was May (Mary Isobel) Cumbrae-Stewart. (The name Cumbrae had been added to Stewart early in the century by the eldest son, Francis, his brothers and sisters being persuaded (after his father's death in 1904) to adopt a rather

Mary Isobel (May) Stewart who would make a number of visits to her cousins in Christchurch.

Courtesy Heather Murchison.

obscure historic connection of the name Cumbrae to the Stewart family). May is said to have made frequent trips to New Zealand usually staying at Riccarton House with Edith Deans, her cousin. Molly's younger brother Reggie was married in 1920 and his wife 'Moll' (née Donald) used, she wrote, to see a lot of May, who loved taking her baby son Robin (born 1931) for walks in his pushchair in Christchurch.

Whether any others of the first family in Melbourne had visited their cousins (the third family) at Riccarton House has not been recorded. From what one can glean they were all busy with their Australian careers and marriages. No later Deans visits are known except one in 1921, when Bill Deans accompanied his sister Maisie to Hong Kong and England. He returned via Melbourne, where he had a happy and profitable visit with his cousin Janet Cumbrae Stewart. She was the youngest child (born 1883) of Bill's Aunt Agnes (his mother's half-sister) and six years younger than Bill.

Janet Cumbrae Stewart. She never used a hyphen in her surname as did other Stewart children.

Courtesy Gillian Webster.

A talented woman (who like her older sister, May, would not marry), her reputation was well established as a 'pastellist'. In fact, in 1916, she was a full member of the Australian Artists Association, 'a prestige usually conferred on the elite of male artists'. Bill caught her just in time. The following year, 1922, she had moved to London, her younger sister Bea accompanying her. She lost many of her works in transit, but Bill came home to New Zealand with three pastels – 'Choose what you would like' she had generously told him, and gave him a book on her art signed by her 'To Cousin Bill'. Lucky man. In London, at her first exhibition there in 1923, Queen Mary, enchanted with the pastels, bought several of her works. Bea came back to Melbourne but Janet was to travel and live in Europe, returning after 17 years to Melbourne in 1939 where she would stay until her death in 1960.

Their mother, Agnes, had died in February 1927 at the age of 83 and the oldest son Francis Cumbrae-Stewart had died in 1938. An account of Agnes' early life in New Zealand appeared in March in the *Lyttelton Times*, written by this son (then Garrick Professor of Law at the University of Queensland). The article ended 'Mrs Stewart never forgot her native country, and it was her wish that she should be remembered in the land she loved'. With Agnes' passing the only surviving child of the five born to Robert and Mary Anne Park, the last direct link with the first family, was gone.

Agnes had been hostess at Montrose at Brighton Beach to many New Zealand friends and relatives over the years up to the end of 1923 when the house was sold. Welcome were the Bannatynes. Aunt Bannatyne, as she was called, was Mary Anne Park's sister, Jane Emily, who after her first husband Richard Baker died, had married Will Bannatyne. Aunt Bannatyne's daughter Emily Cecilia Baker would marry John Kinross, who was the widower of Agnes' sister Mary Jane. Emily Cecilia was a first cousin of Jane Emily. A very close knit family! Then there had been the visit of Marion Park to her stepdaughter Agnes, and Marion's grandson, Bill Deans, the recipient of the pastels. Much earlier there had been a visit of a niece of Robert Park's mother Catherine Lang Park. This was a Mrs. Sands who

Janet Cumbrae Stewart's talent as a pastellist is well known. Queen Mary bought some of her work. Bill Deans was lucky enough to be given three when visiting her in Melbourne. His daughter-in-law, June Deans, now cherishes them in her Christchurch home. Here is one of them.

Courtesy June Deans.

left the Stewart family in Melbourne a memento, a sampler done by Ellen Eliza Sands embroidered 13 December 1869, thus reviving the Scottish connection. No doubt all who came to Montrose would have enjoyed staying with Granny Stewart, for she was, as a granddaughter wrote, 'the dearest person, loved by all her family'.

Agnes Stewart's half-sister Edith Deans became the chatelaine of Riccarton House after the death in 1911 of her mother-in-law Jane Deans. A little more formidable than her half-sister Agnes, she was nevertheless to continue the long tradition of opening Riccarton House to friends, visitors and relatives. There was her sister Minnie Symes and her family to visit and be visited. (Austen Deans tells of these Sunday visits after church of the two sisters. 'After lunch the talk would turn to argument and they would part quite frostily, Sunday after Sunday the pattern would be repeated.') Then of course, her niece Molly Park was in Edith's care as a guardian until 1913, and possibly Molly's brother Reggie Park from time to time. And the visits from across the Tasman of May Cumbrae-Stewart. Perhaps these last ceased in 1937 when Edith died aged 81. Minnie had died the year before aged 78. With Edith's passing all of Robert and Marion Park's children (the third family) had gone.

Following the First World War, when Edith and John Deans' son Alexander (Alister) lost his life, his widow Norah with her two boys Austen and David moved just down the road from Riccarton House.

The inscription to Bill Deans is in a book on his cousin Jan Cumbrae Stewart's art, given to him in 1921 in Melbourne.
Courtesy June Deans.

Granny Stewart, beloved by all, in the drawing room of Montrose.
Courtesy Gillian Webster.

A hand-tinted photo of Robert Park hanging in Riccarton House.

Courtesy Riccarton Bush Trust.

Austen, now, in 2009, aged 94, speaks of spending a great deal of time in his second home with his loved grandmother.

By 1939 Molly (née Park) and Ken Murchison had shifted in to Christchurch from Glenthorne. Bobs Murchison, their son, wrote in an Appendix to the story of Lake Coleridge, that the 'cottage' at Lake Coleridge homestead was burned down. The date of the fire is uncertain. It was probably some time between 1914 and 1916 when Bobs Murchison was born in the Lake Coleridge homestead. 'Regrettably Robert Park's dairies and all his equipment and belongings were … destroyed' in the conflagration. A sad loss of precious records and artifacts, including I am told, Maori carvings.

At Montrose and Riccarton House had hung the photo of Robert Park in his tartan. The copy which the Stewarts in Melbourne had was thought, until recently, to be that of Captain Thomas Stewart, Agnes' husband Francis Stewart's father! That at Riccarton House was always known as the Deans' maternal grandfather. It must have been a great surprise to the Deans and Park descendants to see accompanying an article which appeared in the *Free Lance* in 1939, as a precursor to the 1940 Centennial celebrations, their ancestor's photo, and to read all about their cousins, the Loves and the Bennetts. Denial, and World War II, put any exploration of the relationship on hold. It would not be pursued with any dedication until the 1980s. However, it is only through the lives of the Maori descendants of Robert Park and Terenui, the second family, that the frame is expanded.

CHAPTER 14

AHUREWA CHURCH & TAUMATA – THE SECOND FAMILY

W hen Huta came to the old Maori settlement at Taiaroa Head to join his sister in about 1869/70 there was a church there and a school. It is not at all clear where Anihaka, who had been with her Aunt Koraraina since around 1857, was, even whether she was still living at the Maori village.

Her daughter Ripeka would write in 1939 of an (unnamed) minister and his wife for whom Anihaka worked being very good to her after her aunt died. Although a great-grandson was once shown Koraraina's grave there is no tombstone now in the urupa. Perhaps she rests in the urupa near her husband Taiaroa (who died in 1863) or close to her father Makore Ngatata-i-te-rangi the famed Te Atiawa chief who had died on a visit to his daughter in 1854.

The Otakou Marae at Taiaroa Head. The urupa lies behind the wharenui Tamatea.

Photo Frank Easdale.

Makore Ngatata, it may be recalled, after the siege of Ngamotu Pā in New Plymouth, (Chapter 11) had emigrated with a hikoi southwards to Otaki, Wellington and Queen Charlotte Sound. Ngatata had been a party to the sale of Wellington lands to the New Zealand Company and had relinquished his position as a paramount chief in favour of his son, Wi Tako Ngatata, in 1842. Wi Tako's grandson (and Makore Ngatata's great grandson), Wi Hapi Love, would marry Ripeka, Anihaka's daughter.

The missionary couple who were good to Anihaka may have been the much loved Wesleyan missionaries the Riemenschneiders. In 1868 a railing was being put around the Rev. Riemenschneider's grave, and after his death only a visiting missioner came once a month to minister to the local people, a Maori catechist supplying on the site services until 1877. The mission had been going to be discontinued in 1872 but Hori Kerei (George Grey) Taiaroa, a son born 1844 by a former wife of Taiaroa, had pressed in 1872 for the Methodist Church to continue the work and in 1874 a wharenui was also built. Hori Kerei Taiaroa would, by 1884, be a member of the Legislative

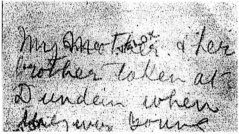

Anihaka and Huta Park. Sister and brother reunited in Otago

The note on the back of the photo is in the hand of Ripeka Love, Anihaka's daughter.

Misc. MS 184/1974 Hocken Library University of Otago.

The view from the urupa looking over the roofs of the marae buildings to the Otago Heads. Huta when he lived at the Kainga was an assistant pilot who guided ships into the harbour.

Photo Frank Easdale.

Council. Now in 1871, when Huta was living at the Heads, H.K. Taiaroa had already been elected a member of the House of Representatives for Southern Maori.

Huta, who it was said had not worn European clothing until he left Taranaki, now donned seaman's garb to be an assistant pilot on the boats which guided visiting ships through the changing channels of the Otago Harbour to a safe berth at Port Chalmers, or on to Dunedin. From 1863 there had been constant requests to the Provincial Council from the Harbourmaster to have young men sufficiently trained as pilots; that they should have had two years at sea, and then be articled for two years. There had been no such training for Huta. The pilot staff who manned the boats, too, had been reduced progressively from 1866, when there were seven, to, in 1868, only four. A steam tug was needed, as, fumed Captain William Thomson, 'the Pilot Service is wrought at a disadvantage with open boats'. In 1870 'occasional pilots' had to be employed as required and Huta was one of these. Thomson wrote again to the Provincial Council begging for a steam tug. 'What the Pilots and their boats' crew earn is with the hazard of their lives in the open boats at present in use at the Heads.' The boat crew earned

£120 p.a. as permanent employees. It seems Huta may have been called in frequently 'to overtake the work' when demand exceeded supply of pilots, but such a system, where they didn't hold a pilot's license, 'should not be continued'. It appears, however, to have been continued up until 1877. Although the Otago Harbour Board had been constituted in 1874, it wasn't until 1877 that authority over piloting was transferred to the Board. The shipping records are missing from 1874 through 1877 but there is a 1874 note of Huta's being engaged in the boat. By 1877, though, Huta was in Motueka getting married.

Huta and Anihaka had left Otago some time in 1875/76 and had come north to Wellington. Here Huta was told by his whanau he was to marry. The wife chosen for him was Pare, or Merenako Kitakita. Pare (or Polly) sometimes called Mere (Mary) was from Golden Bay in the Aorere locality, but had been at Motueka Church of England Boarding School from the age of 13. The school was run by Mr and Mrs Baker. Baker was a son of the Bay of Islands missionary who had come to New Zealand in 1828, and was consequently a fluent Maori speaker. The school was connected through to the Baker's house by a kitchen with a combined dining and school room adjoining, and a dormitory over. According to the inspector in 1876, it was discouraging work teaching the children. Parents would complain of lack of progress but wouldn't permit them to be punished if they neglected their lessons. The plain sewing and fancy work were beautifully executed by the girls and they could recite reams of poetry remarkably well. The girls were evidently biddable and besides learning the three R's and History, studied Geography, Music and Scripture along with the boys, as was the practice in Anglican boarding schools at that time. They were also expected to do domestic training, that is cooking, cleaning and making and mending their clothes. But the boys wouldn't have a bar of it, one father taking his son away when told by him that he was made to chop firewood for the school-room fire. Why should the boy work when the 'great' revenue from the endowment was sufficient to pay for labour? The revenue from the church land could in fact support only a small number of pupils, and the school was running with a deficit which had been met by the Bishop of Nelson. Pare Kitakita had done well at school to the pride of her father's childless cousin, Mere Nako, whose

Merenako or Pare (Polly) Kitakita (seated) and
her sister in Nelson. Lying across her lap could
be the kiwi feather cloak which was passed
down through the female line.

18850/3 Nelson Provincial Museum.

Mere Nako, who adopted her cousin Kitakita's
daughter Pare (Polly) with her famous kahu-
kiwi and tiki. The greenstone tiki is now in the
care of the Nelson Museum.

Courtesy Mairangi Reiher.

name Pare had taken when 'adopted' by the old lady. Hoani Kitakita, it is said, had
not wanted her to go to Mere Nako, fearing that she would become a virtual slave to
the old woman and he would not speak to Mere Nako for some years. Did he see the
school report of 1875? Of the seven girls and three boys, Polly was second in the three
R's and in sewing third. 'Polly excels in cutting out and general work, but is not so neat
in sewing.'

Pare would have been only 16 when she married Huta at St Thomas' church at
Motueka on 30 August 1877. Huta hadn't wanted to get married but he was after all
27, and bowed to his elders' wishes.

The bride had four bridesmaids and was in white with veil and wreath, much like the European style of her Pakeha cousin Edith Deans (née Park) in 1879. The marriage celebrant was the Rev. T.S. Grace, the Bishop's Maori chaplain. The wedding breakfast was in the 20 by 14 foot schoolroom where the Bakers hosted the gathering of 60 people. Here was Hoani Kitakita, (was all forgiven?) who thanked the company for their kind interest in his daughter's welfare. Further, he felt it a great compliment to have so many Pakeha at the wedding. He'd been skeptical about the Pakeha profession of goodwill; now he was convinced it was true. The happy result seen in his daughter Pare had decided him to send another daughter to the school. Not to be outdone his cousin, old Mere Nako, made an animated speech. She could not say too much in praise of the Pakeha. Here was a manifestation of their goodness and love to Maori. Long live the Pakeha! Long live the Bishop of Nelson, who had sent a tangible proof of his affection – this silver teapot should accompany the bride and bridegroom on their wedding tour, and be shown to all their relatives in this and in the North Island. She sat down to loud and prolonged cheering. The rift between the cousins was apparently healed, and the Bakers could be proud of one of their oldest pupils. Sadly this school and the Bakers were not to stay beyond 1880 and the Whakarewa Trust took over, with scholarships offered. An 'Industrial School' would be established.

A tale chuckled over by descendants is this: because Huta hadn't wanted to be wed the marriage wasn't consummated for a year – but then once started, they couldn't stop! They were to have, from 1879 to 1898, eleven children. Of these only five would survive to adulthood.

It was another matter for Huta's sister, Anihaka. She had been joined in the Maori way in Petone to Paati Matene, eight years younger than she. Paati, or Patrick, was the son of Matene Tauwhare and Roka (Rose) Te Puni. Roka's father, Honiana Te Puni, was the Petone chief who with Wharepouri had welcomed the New Zealand Company settlers to his land in 1839, among them Robert Park, his wife Mary Anne and her sister Emily Jane. Now, when this daughter of his second family was joined to the great chief, Robert Park was forever more closely bonded to Te Atiawa. Te Puni and Robert Park had died in the same year, 1870, Robert in March and Honiana Te Puni, in December.

Above: Paati Matene (son of Matene Tauwhare and grandson of Te Puni) who married Anihaka Park. They had one child, Ripeka.
Courtesy Peter Love.

Left: Matene Tauwhare, husband of Roka Te Puni and father of Paati Matene.
Courtesy Peter Love.

Robert rests in Christchurch. Te Puni at the urupa in Te Puni Street Petone, where Terenui, Anihaka and Huta's mother, also lies, buried it is said by Pare Kitakita's father, Hoani Kitakita, Huta's father-in-law.

For some reason unknown to the family the famous name which Patrick had inherited from his father was dropped and he was known as Paati Matene, not Patrick Tauwhare. He had been, however, still known as Patrick Tauwhare when Wi Tako Ngatata died on 6 November 1887. The funeral was huge; 4,000 – 5,000 people attended. The Legislative Council (of which Ngatata had been a member since 1872) adjourned as a mark of respect. Taniora (Daniel) Love, married to Wi Tako's only child

Hohepine, was a chief mourner and Paati Matene was close by. Paati was 31 and already with Anihaka, and the little Wi Hapi Pakau Love (son of Taniora and Hohepine) whom their daughter Ripeka, five years old at this time, would one day marry was beside Paati. A eulogy recalled Dr. Featherston as saying 'Wi Tako is the cleverest man, black or white, in the country'. Nobody, of course, would mention Robert Park and his close association with Wi Tako as a neighbour, their buying negotiations in Hawkes Bay, and that Wi Tako was said to have 'given' Terenui to Robert Park.

Matene became Anihaka's married surname, but she and Patrick were not married under European law until 6 December 1888 in the Registry Office in Wellington. It may have been from then

Ripeka with her mother, Anihaka Matene (née) Park.

Courtesy Peter Love.

that the 'Tauwhare' was dropped? Patrick's profession, on the marriage certificate, is given as 'Farmer' and he is 32. Ani has '40' but as mentioned before she probably didn't know her exact age and she may have been at least some months younger. They had tried for a number of years for children and of those born all had died in infancy.

At last a tohunga advised them to go away from the mainland and so they went to Kapiti Island where their only surviving child, Ripeka, was born on 28 June 1882. This precious child, adored by her mother Ani and in turn greatly loved by her child, was destined because of her aristocratic Maori heritage, to be married to another distinguished Te Atiawa family – the Loves. The Loves were descended from John (Jacky) Agar Love, the Scottish trader turned whaler, who had been in Taranaki. He had gone

Left: Ripeka in her wedding gown on the day she married Wi Hapi Love in St James Church, Lower Hutt. Hana Park, her cousin from Motueka was a bridesmaid.

Courtesy Peter Love.

The newly weds. Ripeka and Wi Hapi Love.

Courtesy Peter Love.

south with the Te Atiawa hikoi, and had lived and died in the Marlborough Sounds. From the union of Jacky Love with Hikanui, had come the grandson Taniora (Daniel) Love who married Wi Tako Ngatata's only child Hohepine (Josephine). The marriage of their son, Wi Hapi Pakau Love, to Ripeka Matene, would strengthen the ancient links.

Ripeka Matene and Wi Hapi Love were married at St James Anglican Church, Lower Hutt on 14 December 1897. The church bell rang out in celebration; the bell of the ship *Sobraon* which had been retrieved by Sir William Fitzherbert from the ship-wreck of 1848. Then, the Fitzherberts had had in their care Robert Park's daughters Mary Jane and Agnes of his first family, and were on their way to England when the vessel was wrecked. There were 2,000 guests from both South and North Islands at the

Taumata, the house
that Ripeka and Wi
Hapi built on Korokoro
Hill above Petone.
Courtesy Peter Love.

Love/Matene wedding, Maori and Pakeha. But following the wedding reception, very sadly, Ripeka's father Paati Matene died suddenly. Seemingly the strain of events had been too much, and the planned evening ball was cancelled. Mother Ani Matene (née Park) would die a year later on 27 August 1898. She lies next to her husband and near her mother Terenui at Te Puni Urupa in Petone. Ripeka was to recall her mother in a letter of 1939. 'My mother [Anihaka] was so refined and should have had better luck out of life in the good things of this world but she herself would not have (chosen this), for she was loved and looked up to by all around her, she taught my Father's people to read and write even to pray both she and uncle [Huta] were true servants of God. A good woman and the best mother in all the world.'

Ripeka and Patrick's first home was in Queen Charlotte Sound farming on the family property Home Bush at East Bay on Arapawa Island. They would have ten children, three of whom died in infancy. In 1911 they returned to the North Island and built their home Taumata on the Korokoro Hill overlooking Petone, where Robert Park had landed in 1840. Below was the old pā site on the Western Hutt Road, where Petone West Primary School would be built and Ripeka and Wi Hapi's children had their early

Dave Raukawa Park, youngest son of Huta and Pare Park, at Taumata where he lived with his cousin Ripeka for a time.

Godber Album Photographic Coll. APG-0682 A.T.L.

education, and later the Te Tatau-o-te-Po Marae which celebrated its 75th year in 2000. Wi Hapi had a large estate in the Waiwhetu, where much of the land was leased, and they were very comfortably off. Their large eight-bedroomed home was always open to family, and here, about two years after the house was built, David Raukawa Park, the baby of Huta and Pare's family in Motueka, at 15 or so, came to live with his cousin Ripeka while working out an apprenticeship as a fitter and turner at the railway workshops in Petone.

Dave Park had been born in Motueka in November 1898, a year after Ripeka and Wi Hapi were wed. His oldest sister, and Huta and Pare's first-born, Hana Te Unuhi Park, was 18 and had been a bridesmaid to Ripeka. It was at this wedding, it is said, that she and the young minister, the Rev. Fredrick Bennett of Te Arawa tribe (Rotorua) fell in love. Fred Bennett had been priested in November 1897. He had been one of the first to receive his Licentiate in Theology at the newly founded Theological College in Nelson.

1897 had been a notable year for the Maori of Motueka. The devoted Christian followers had raised a new church Ahurewa inspired by Huta Park and newly ordained Fred Bennett. This replaced Amate, or Blind River Church, a tiny wooden building with a belfry, narrow lancet windows, a railed-in Communion table, a reading desk and a pulpit 'only a man of spare habit could have occupied'. It was at this old church, however, where 'the borer held hands' that the funeral service for Pare's Kuia,

Huta Pamariki Park and Pare with their four children. Harry the oldest boy with the dog, his older sister Hana in front of her mother, with Wikitoria lying in front. Huta nurses the baby Dave.

Courtesy Athalie Watt.

Mere Nako, was held following her death at Huta and Pare's home where she then lived. Mere Nako's age was given as 90. Some said she was 105. Her casket, followed by relatives, was taken to the urupa down the road, where this old lady from the Taranaki hapu Puketapu of Ngati Ruanui (Titokowaru's tribe) had her rest.

In 1874 thousands of acres of land in south Taranaki had been sold. The hapu received at the hand of their cousin Wi Tako Ngatata, monies for the purchase. This was divided amongst many, including Mere Nako, her cousin Hoani Kitakita, Oriwia Paruka (Pare's

Ahurewa Church, Motueka, raised by the joint efforts of Huta Park and the Rev. Frederick Bennett. Opening day – a proud day when boatloads of people came from Nelson. Huta and Pare can be seen in front of the door at left.

Courtesy Athalie Watt.

maternal grandmother) and Huria (Julia) Matenga (famous as the Grace Darling of New Zealand for her part in the rescue of those on the ship *Delaware* in 1863). Those named in this deed had other small sums too from lands sold in the Marlborough Sounds.

Pare inherited from Mere Nako most of her land at Motueka, that is, the land which the Park's farmed as well as that on long term leases. Huta also inherited from the Kuia, but much less. In the same year that Mere Nako died, a daughter Wikitoria was born to Huta and Pare. In between the two girls was Harry, born in 1886. Hana and Wiki were sent to Hukarere Maori Girls' School in Napier, while Harry spent time at Te Aute College near Hastings.

Hana had seen quite a bit of Fred Bennett before the Petone wedding of Ripeka and Wi Hapi, when he and her father Huta (a synodsman for the Nelson Anglican diocese) had worked to raise Ahurewa Church. It had been a grand all-day celebration in May 1897 when the church opened. Boatloads came from Nelson to fill two marquees where they feasted on the food from the huge hangi put down. The dedication service was held out of doors, with the Bishop of Nelson, assisted by Archdeacon Grace, and the Revs Kempthorne, Baker, Chatterton, Johnston and Bennett presiding. Hemi Matenga (Huria's husband) and Huta Paaka on behalf of Maori made speeches of thanks. It was Huta who gave the name to the Church 'Ahurewa, The Sacred Place'. However, Hana Park and Fred Bennett were married 11 May 1899, in St Thomas Church, as Hana's father and mother Huta and Pare had been in 1877.

Far left: Looking from the altar rail to the back of Te Ahurewa. On the left is the encased Union Jack, given to the Motueka people for their loyalty to the Crown.

Photo John Wilson.

Left: The carved altar table was given to Te Ahurewa in it's Jubilee year of 1947 by Bishop Frederick Bennett in memory of his wife, Hana Paaka.

Photo John Wilson.

The memorial tablet to Huta and Mere Paaka.

Photo Frank Easdale.

Te Ahurewa from the road. Trees, memorials to Bishop Bennett and Nelson Synodsman Huta Park, shade the church. A rata and a totara were planted by Huta, a native cedar (kaiwaka) and rata by Fred Bennett. The church has a Category 2 New Zealand Historic Places Trust rating.

Photo Frank Easdale.

Te Awhina Marae next to Te Ahurewa.

Photo Frank Easdale.

217

The youthful Hana and Frederick Bennett.

26952/3 Nelson Provincial Museum.

It is told that Wiki fell in love at this wedding with Fred's brother Harry Bennett. If it is true, then Wiki at 11 was unknowingly following her Pakeha cousin, Minnie (Robert Park's third family), in choosing a husband at the tender age of 11! But marry him she did, in time, and was to live in Wellington in Hawkestone Street. Harry Bennett, a Wellington merchant, was a City Councillor and Deputy Mayor for a time, and Chairman of the Works Committee of the Wellington City Council.

Hana and Fred Bennett went first to Taranaki on the Bell Block. Then Fred was Chaplain to the Bishop of Auckland for two years and from Auckland went to Rotorua. Here Fred was back home at last in Te Arawa territory. The Bennetts by then had three children born in Taranaki. Their last child, before the tragedy of Hana Bennett's death, was born on 12 June 1909. Hana died on the 10 August and was laid to rest in a tomb near the entrance to St Faith's Church on Lake Rotorua. Huta and Pare came north to mourn the death of their beloved eldest daughter, taking back with them their two-month-old granddaughter, Hannah Moari Bennett, to be reared by them in Motueka. Their youngest child Dave was 11. Hana Park had not lived to see her husband become the first Bishop of Aotearoa – and the first Maori Bishop. Young Hannah Bennett, however, would be so aware of her famous father every time she went into Ahurewa which he and her grandfather had been responsible for raising. In fact she told her daughters that, as they spent a lot of time at the church and because the family always kept the old chalice made of totara wood at their homestead, Hannah as a child thought Ahurewa belonged to her family.

In the church was a reminder of the days of Titokowaru, Te Whiti, and Parihaka Pā in Taranaki. A flag, a Union Jack, had been presented to the Motueka people in 1863 in recognition of their loyalty to the Crown at the time of the Taranaki Wars. Relations, refugees from the troubled territory of Taranaki, had at one time tried to persuade their cousins to join them and go north to fight the Pakeha colonists, but they would not. The flagpole was chopped down. The flag was rescued and hidden but is now displayed in a case on the wall of Ahurewa. Huta had long turned away from conflict but was sympathetic to the plight of his relations at Parihaka. Eels and mussels were dried, and potatoes were packed and sent up to the pā.

The congregation at Motueka was fed after services at Ahurewa at the homestead of Huta and Pare. The homestead is gone now, burned down in 1939, but descendants hold in memory the canopy of cherry trees arching over the tables laid to feed the people who came to stay or were living with them. Huta was remembered as saying to granddaughter Hannah Bennett, 'You know if it wasn't for your Momma and her thirty-two dependents I'd be a wealthy man'. There was no marae at Motueka then and the Park home acted as one in gathering the hapu together.

Another granddaughter, Athalie, recalled the hop kiln on the property. Her father Dave, the youngest of Huta and Pare's children, was living there in 1939 when the house burned. Pare outlived Huta, (who died in 1927) by 11 years. She had lived with her son Dave and wife Dulcie until her passing in 1938. Her granddaughter Athalie remembered so well her Granny Park weaving flax boxes to use in hangi and for school lunches, drying eels, and grinding well boiled and dried karaka berries to make flour. Much of their inheritance through Granny Park of taonga of piupiu, huia feathers and paintings was lost in the fire, but Dulcie, Dave's wife, rescued the photos, while Dave saved the kiwi feather cloak which had been old Mere Nako's. This cloak is passed down from senior daughter to senior daughter and with Athalie's death in 2007, is in the care of her daughter Jane. After the fire, Ahurewa Church became the focus of the people of Mouteka and is now central to Te Awhina Marae which enfolds it.

Outside the barn at Motueka on the Park property where the hops and later tobacco was dried. Bearded Huta holds infant Dave, while eldest son Harry leans over them. Is it Wiki on the horse?

Courtesy Athalie Watt.

Left: Eeling. A river picnic at Motueka. Huta holds the eel pot. Hana Park and Fred Bennett are beside him on the right. Holding the rifle behind Huta is Harry Park and in front of her father is Wikitoria.

Courtesy Athalie Watt.

Above: Aunty Wiki Bennett, a much loved and respected Wellington identity.

Courtesy Julie Temple.

Left: 'Mr Tama', the walking stick carved by Wikitoria's father, Huta Park, for his granddaughter June who was crippled by polio as a child. Wikitoria Bennett, June's mother, was a founder of the Crippled Children's Society in Wellington.

Photo James Wheeler.

Back in Wellington in 1939, when the Motueka homestead burned, Wiki Bennett (née Park) with her husband Harry was living in Hawkestone Street in the city. Out in Petone was her cousin Ripeka Love (née Matene) at Taumata. They both led distinguished lives. Both were recipients of the O.B.E, Wikitoria for welfare work with Maori. She was a founder of Ngati Poneke Association, a founding member of the Crippled Children's Society and had worked for many years for the Y.W.C.A. Aunty Wiki, as she came to be known to a host of people, was 'a darling' of both Maori and Pakeha and sadly missed when she died in 1975.

Ripeka had been rewarded with the O.B.E. in 1919 for her patriotic and welfare work in the First World War. She, too, and husband Wi Hapi (who would also receive an O.B.E. in 1949) would support Ngati Poneke. Ripeka had said in a 1939 letter that life was 'just a bustle' there was so much to be done. She and Wi Hapi had 14 beautiful grandchildren, and she was busy with a daughter teaching Maori girls weaving, and this 'wonderful' work would be shown alongside that of their Pakeha sisters in a space set aside at the Centennial Exhibition in 1940 – a celebration of the signing of the Treaty of Waitangi. Also Petone was to be the scene of celebrations of the centenary of the landings of the new settlers, including Ripeka's Pakeha forebear, Robert Park. The Loves gave money to help build the memorial to early settlers on the Petone foreshore and Ripeka had been a member of the Hutt Valley Centennial Committee and Wi Hapi was chairman of the local Maori Centennial Committee.

It was hardly surprising then that reporters interviewed the Love family, and that in both the *Dominion* in Wellington, and the *Free Lance*, articles appeared in which Ripeka's Maori/Pakeha heritage was described. The *Free Lance* went around the country. In Dunedin another, but later, emigrant from Scotland, would read it. The consequence? Mungo Park's trunk was dispatched north to find a home with the Love's at Taumata. How this came to be is revealed in Chapter 16.

CHAPTER 15

FAMILY MISUNDERSTANDINGS

The article in the *Free Lance* was full of errors about Ripeka's Pakeha forebears, a mixture of lack of knowledge about Robert Park's early life and the free interpretation by the reporter of what the Love's had told her. Robert Park was said to have come from 'a good Inverness family'.

How the Loves had got hold of this notion is a mystery. But Inverness was the Scottish city which the descendants of Park's third family also had as a place where Robert's mother went to after leaving Glasgow and where she died. She didn't. The mistake was made by descendants assuming that a photo taken of Little Kate's gravestone by an Inverness photographer meant the grave must also be in Inverness. A later photo shows the names of Robert Park's sisters have been added. Again, it was thought, that this grave had to be in Inverness. The first family however had the grave site right; it was in London. The only connection with Inverness was through Robert's sculptor brother Patric's wife Robina Carruthers who had lived in Inverness before her marriage.

Robert Park was further said to have first surveyed in Australia under the Macquarrie Government before coming to New Zealand, when he met Terenui, a Hawera 'chieftainess'. When his time expired, Park's intention was to take his wife and daughter back home, 'but Maori tradition forbade the women's departure'. They were hidden and

Ripeka and Wi Hapi Love. The photo which headed the *Free Lance* article 18 January 1933, titled 'The Loves of Petone'. In the article is a photo of Robert Park, Ripeka Love's grandfather.

when he returned years later from the United Kingdom he was still unable to find them. Not much here that was right! For instance Macquarrie died five years before Park first set sail! There was not a mention of Anihaka's brother Huta.

This article was either seen by or drawn to the attention of a Miss Gladys Currie of Waingoro Springs, near Mosgiel, south of Dunedin. She corresponded in that year, 1939, and again in 1940 with Ripeka Love. Wikitoria Bennett's husband, Henry Bennett, was in touch with Miss Currie's brother. Unfortunately none of Miss Currie's letters or those of her brother seem to have survived, but those from Ripeka Love and

Henry Bennett were kept by Miss Currie and are in the Hocken Library in Dunedin. Also kept was a hand-written account of Robert Park, and of his second (Maori) family written in Wellington, also in 1939, by Harry Park, Huta's eldest son. Far from correcting or clarifying the history given in the *Free Lance* article, errors were compounded. What Harry Park drew on to write this is unknown. Stories half remembered, and woven to a colourful tangle, so imaginatively. And as often is the case, these myths handed down, were thought to be facts by a later generation.

By 1939 there was no one to check Harry's work. He was the senior surviving member, at 53, of Huta Park's family. Huta had died in 1927, his wife in 1938 and Harry's older sister Hana Bennett in 1909. Wiki Bennett was a couple of years younger than Harry and perhaps unlikely to quarrel with Harry's account even if she thought it wrong. Certainly in her old age, she knew that Robert Park had not gone back to Scotland, but had perhaps been away surveying at the time Terenui had died in December 1850. Ripeka Love seems to have largely accepted Harry's account of Robert's early life, although there are differences in later events.

Harry Park's account is extraordinary. First of all he has Robert Park working and waiting in Australia for his wife to arrive. They'd evidently been busy before leaving Scotland, producing five children, all girls. Two were left at boarding school – in Inverness. The steamer failed to 'take the right course on entering Sydney Harbour'. Instead of turning left it went straight onto the land and was wrecked. Park's wife and a daughter were drowned. This left two daughters, one of whom, he wrote, married a McDonald in Sydney. After about a year Robert comes to New Zealand. There is often a hint of a truth, a fact, in such accounts, and it could be that Harry had heard of Park's two daughters of his first family surviving the wreck of the *Sobraon* in 1848 at Wellington Harbour Heads, when the pilot 'missed stays'. Anyway, Robert according to Harry, would have been free to marry Terenui right from his arrival in New Zealand. in early 1840. Well he wasn't (he was still married to Mary Anne), and he couldn't have been married as Harry supposes by Octavius Hadfield at that time, nor later, and no church registers were burnt as he contends. Later on, in the 'Bennett Saga' (an unpublished Bennett family document about Bishop Fredrick Bennett and compiled in the 1970s) pieces of

Park history have been added in because of the Bishop's first marriage to Hana Park. It is recounted that there was a chance meeting with the Methodist Rev. Pratt who knew of marriage and birth records in the Methodist Archive relating to the Parks. There is no Methodist record of a marriage to be found, and the christening of a son, jubilantly seized upon as being a child of Robert Park and Terenui, is in fact that of Patric Park born to Robert's first wife Mary Anne in Port Chalmers, Otago in 1846.

Harry Park's account then follows the fortunes of Terenui and Robert Park's children to Taranaki and to Otago Heads. He finishes with the information that Park, 'later married a pakeha woman said to be his housekeeper. From this marriage came one son and at least two daughters'. He has the two daughters married off correctly to Dr Symes and John Deans II. But the son he says, 'became Prof. G. Park of the Otago University who is the father of A.D. Park of the Treasury'. This is perhaps a confusion with Prof. James Park who in 1882 went to Nelson where he worked for several years as a computing geologist for the Survey Department and was later professor at Otago before going to Thames. The error crops up again in the 'Bennett Saga'. The son of course was surveyor/engineer Robert George Park.

With the 1939 *Free Lance* article, a photo appeared. The caption read, 'Mrs Love's Highland grandfather, Robert Park, surveyor from Inverness, whose son became Governor of New South Wales and was knighted'. Goodness me! Robert Park was never so grand. Moreover, in the article Robert Park has also been elevated to being 'a nephew of Mungo Park, the explorer, and of Matthew Park, whose grandson was a famous sculptor of Victorian days'. There is not one thing which is correct here. Glasgow-born Matthew Park was Robert and Patric Park's (the sculptor's) father. Certainly a Robert Park was a nephew of Mungo Park but as was shown in Chapter 2 he was of the Selkirk Parks, not the Glasgow Parks. Nevertheless, the descendants of Robert Park's second family firmly believed in the Selkirk relationship. It was repeated in the 'Bennett Saga' where the explorer Mungo Park has been knighted by the writer. He is now Sir Mungo Park, the great-great-grandfather of Hana Bennett (née Park). Then Sir Mungo is given two sons, Matthew (alleged to be Hana's great-grandfather) and Alexander. Curiously Patrick Park, the true great-great-grandfather of Hana did have a Matthew and an

The sculpture by Andrew Currie of James Hogg, the Borders Poet, at St Mary's Loch.

Photo Heather Murchison.

Andrew Currie was known for his passion for The Borders country and its history. In August 1883 he led a party on an 'Excursion up the Yarrow' and an article on the excursion appeared in a magazine of the Berwickshire Naturalists Club. Andrew Currie had grown up at Howford on the Ettrick, just over the low hills which separated the valleys of the Yarrow River and Ettrick Water. Andrew's father was William Currie who was a tenant farmer of Howford, of the land-owner the Duke of Buccleuch, as was Mungo Park's father, also named Mungo Park, at Foulshiels on the Yarrow. Andrew's grandfather had also served a Duke of Buccleuch as a factor from about 1760 – 1780.

The connection of Mungo Park, the explorer, to the Currie family came about like this. In Selkirk had long lived the Lang family, and a Mrs Lang, as a girl, had been 'schooled' with the young Mungo. When Mungo came to write of his travels in 1798 he found his Foulshiels home small and crowded, and noisy with farm activities. So in Mrs Lang's house in Selkirk 'he prepared much of his first account of Africa'. Besides which, he was closer there to his 'lovely Allie', Allison Anderson, the doctor's daughter who was to be his wife. In the Lang household, there were also two daughters, Margaret and Henerietta. Margaret would marry Archibald Park, Mungo's older brother in 1799, and later that same year Mungo would marry Allison Anderson. It would be 1810 when Henrietta Lang married William Currie and went up the Ettrick Water to the farm at Howford. Archibald and Margaret Park were then farming nearby, with Isobel, the youngest Park sister, housekeeping for them.

Andrew Currie's well known statue of the explorer Mungo Park in the heart of Selkirk. The base has later sculptural embellishments.

Photo Heather Murchison.

The trunk may have been left in the Lang's house when Mungo went to London. He writes from his sister Peggy Dickson's home to 'Bel' (Isobel) asking 'how Sandy's marriage goes on'. Alexander (Sandy) the younger brother next to Mungo, married Alison Veitch in November 1798, and their tenth child and last born was Robert Park born on 16 October 1812. Andrew Currie and this Robert Park therefore were related (cousins) through his Aunt Margaret's marriage to the Selkirk Parks.

Learning of this Robert Park's birth in Selkirk, confirmed for the second family of Park descendants (Loves, Bennetts and Parks) that their ancestor 'Robert Park' was indeed the nephew of the explorer Mungo Park. A supposition which Miss Currie accepted, especially when she received Harry Park's piece on 'Mungo Park History'.

Henry Bennett in his 1939 letter to Mr Currie referred him to New Zealand publications where he would find 'ample references' to Park's arrival in New Zealand and his survey work in Wellington. The only publication at this time which gives a biography, and a photo, of Robert Park, is Louis Ward's *Early Wellington* (1926).

The Yarrow, which flows down to Selkirk past the ruins of Mungo Park's old house at Foulshiels. Here, sculptor Andrew Currie in 1883 told his stories of the old days of the Borders to those walking with him

Photo Heather Murchison.

The bridge over the Ettrick. The Curries had farmed nearby.

Photo Heather Murchison.

The biographical information on Robert Park, apart from that gleaned from official documents and scattered and fragmentary references in passenger lists and incomplete lists of births and marriages, is from Ripeka Love. Along with other family photographs reproduced in Ward's book is the ubiquitous one of Robert Park. Ripeka in her 1940 letter to Miss Currie, writes that she had lent this photo, given to her mother Anihaka by a friend, to the Parks in Motueka to copy. She feared it was now lost. There is no mention in Ward's short biography of other descendants – of the Pakeha Parks, the Stewarts, the Deans and the Symes, only the Loves and Bennetts.

Henry Bennett finishes his letter to Mr Currie 'Naturally if you can trace any connection as to cousinship with your old people the information would be very useful ... I would be delighted personally to know that such is the case, and that someday we might meet and talk about the peculiar circumstances that has brought Scotland and Maoriland together in this miniature form'.

On 22 June 1939 he had another letter, this time from Mr Currie's sister, Miss Gladys Currie. He intends, he replies, reading her very interesting letter to his wife's sister, Ripeka Love, as soon as he can see

Taumata, the Love homestead. A view from above of the Korokoro hill, and beyond, across the Hutt Valley to the Eastern Hills. The land to the left of Taumata homestead was farmed by Wi Hapi and Ripeka Love.

Courtesy Peter Love.

her. His wife (Wikitoria) is 'looking forward to seeing the famous trunk with all its history and associations ... I was also somewhat intrigued to note that we may be very distantly related to the Melbourne knight Sir Allen Currie'. So they would have been had the Selkirk 'Robert Park' been their forebear, as Sir Allen was the New Zealand Currie's cousin. A son of William Currie and Henrietta Lang, John Lang Currie, a brother of Miss Currie's grandfather Andrew Currie, had emigrated to Australia in 1841. John Lang Currie had two Australian-born sons; another John Lang, and one to become Sir Allen Currie.

'Photographs of some of the descendants of Te Puni, Wi Tako Ngatata, Pomare, and Robert Park, and Barraud's original paintings of Te Puni, Wharepouri, and other, are adorning the Hall (designed as a Maori house) at Mr. Hapi Love's house, Korokoro Hill, Petone.' Louis E. Ward, *Early Wellington* p.393. The reception room at Taumata where taonga surrounded visitors to the hall which was used as a marae.

Courtesy Peter Love.

On a typed copy of Harry Park's 'Mungo Park History' there is written in two columns the supposed relationship of the Park and Currie families, and hence the descent from the Selkirk 'Robert Park'. It has Mungo Park the explorer and Andrew Currie as cousins. This is actually a generation out of step. The Mungo Park here (which evidently Miss Currie has told of) is indeed her grandfather Andrew's cousin, but is not the explorer. He was a son, born in 1801, of the explorer's brother, Archibald, and Margaret (née Lang), and therefore further relationships are mistaken. These notes on the typescript are likely to have been made by David Raukawa Park, the much younger brother of Harry Park, the author of the 'Mungo Park History', both sons of Huta Park.

To return to the correspondence of 1939. Following the two letters written by Henry Bennett comes one further note written by his son to say his father is 'indisposed' but that the trunk had arrived that morning, 5 July 1939, and they wish to thank Miss Currie once again for all the trouble she had gone to on their behalf. The trunk would find a home at Taumata at Petone, Ripeka and Wi Hapi Love's home. They had what was virtually a museum, a reception room which was a repository of taonga – carvings, cloaks, paintings, photographs. Now Mungo Park's trunk joined these treasures and would remain with them until Ripeka Love's death in 1953.

The correspondence with Miss Currie was now continued by Ripeka Love. In October 1939 she sends her thanks for 'the Trunk of Mungo Park it was great of you & I am most grateful for your kind thoughts of the valuable gift and for sending it to me'. She tells Miss Currie her story of Robert Park's going back to Scotland from Wellington, and how he was supposed to have said he would like to send the two children, Anihaka and Huta, back for their schooling – though they would come back to New Zealand. And how afraid Maori were of the children's going, and how they hid them and told Robert Park they had died. This does not tie in with Harry Park's version, who has father Robert giving Wi Tako Ngatata money and telling him 'Above all have them educated'. There had been at least one more letter from Miss Currie, but it was not until a year after Ripeka's earlier reply that Ripeka again wrote back, in October 1940. She apologises, but she has had an operation on her leg, and has been months recovering at a daughter's. The Second World War has begun and she is much involved. She thanks Miss Currie for the guinea sent by her which has been used to buy wool to knit into 'comforts' for the boys overseas. Later, 'My dear I feel very much related to you … one can not help thinking there is a tie of friendship between our families even if it is a long way back'. This sounds as if Ripeka has been made aware of the Currie/Park relationship through the Lang sister marriages, but still assumes that the Selkirk 'Robert Park' is her grandfather. A belief, it seems, which only came to be questioned by some family members in recent years.

Ripeka sends off the photo of her mother Anihaka and uncle Huta taken all those years ago when both sister and brother were in Dunedin. She will also send a photo, she says, of Robert Park's 'Mother and his sister Jean' got by a 'cousin' (Mrs Lightband) in New Zealand from Scotland. 'I wonder if it is the Jean', she asks, 'who gave your people the trunk?'. The photo is lost. Apart from the fact that Surveyor Robert Park didn't have a sister 'Jean', there was no photography of that kind before Park left for New Zealand. I suspect it was one of the series of photos taken in Wellington, some of which are reproduced in Chapter 10. These were of Robert Park with one of his daughters, Mary Jane or Agnes, and may have been sent to relations in Scotland, and had later come back to Mrs Lightband in Nelson. Archibald Park, (Mungo Park, the traveller's, brother) who married Margaret Lang (the sister of Henrietta Currie) had a daughter Jean and it is possible that this is the 'Jean' to whom Miss Currie has referred as giving the trunk to the Curries. Ripeka tells Gladys Currie that her friends say she is 'a very lucky woman to have such a treasure' – the Trunk. 'I tell them an angel sent it to me.'

The 'angel', Gladys Currie, as a young woman, had left from Liverpool for New Zealand in 1912. Mungo Park's trunk had come with her. The Currie family had always known that the trunk had belonged to Mungo Park.

What of the trunk? Where did it come from before it was at Margaret and Henrietta Lang's old home in Selkirk, holding Mungo Park papers, and perhaps other artifacts? The trunk is rather crudely made, constructed of timber of unknown origin, and roughly but sturdily covered in hide, patterned with brass studs. The trunk is taken care of at present at Te Papa Tongarewa the National Museum in Wellington. It is the opinion of the Collections Manager, History, and of a conservator at Te Papa, that the place of manufacture might well have been West Africa, given the Mungo Park history. It may be recalled from Chapter 3 that by the time the traveller had struggled back to Pisania, the place from which he had started out, he had lost almost all his belongings. His friends there rejoiced to see him as they had given him up for dead. His papers fortunately, were safe in his tall beaver hat, his only surviving possession. Perhaps the trunk was made for him there, at Dr. John Laidley's, or he may have been given one already made, but in any event it could have accompanied him back to London, and then on to Scotland and Selkirk.

Where the trunk went after Park left it at the Langs' is not clear, but it is probable, if 'Jean' gave the trunk to the Currie family, that it came to William Currie and Henrietta (née Lang) at Howford, after Jean's father Archibald had died in 1820 on the Isle of Mull. However it came to the Curries, and exactly when, is of no great consequence, though it would be interesting to know. The trunk came to Miss Currie through her great-grandparents William and Henrietta Currie. It passed to their son the sculptor Andrew Currie, appropriately as Andrew Currie sculpted the Selkirk Statue of Mungo Park. The trunk passed then either directly to his granddaughter Gladys Currie, or through Andrew's son George, Gladys' father.

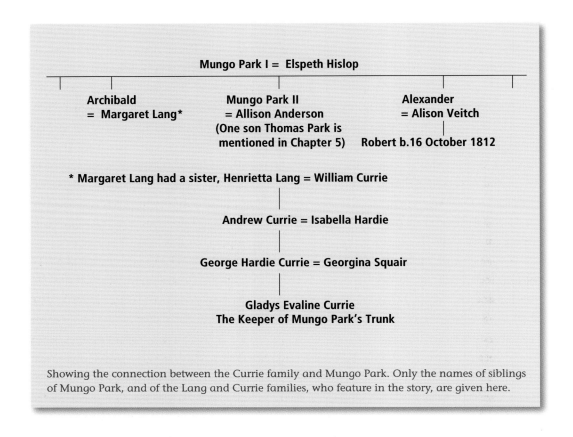

Mungo Park I = Elspeth Hislop

Archibald **= Margaret Lang***	**Mungo Park II** **= Allison Anderson** **(One son Thomas Park is** **mentioned in Chapter 5)**

Alexander
= Alison Veitch

Robert b.16 October 1812

* Margaret Lang had a sister, Henrietta Lang = William Currie

Andrew Currie = Isabella Hardie

George Hardie Currie = Georgina Squair

Gladys Evaline Currie
The Keeper of Mungo Park's Trunk

Showing the connection between the Currie family and Mungo Park. Only the names of siblings of Mungo Park, and of the Lang and Currie families, who feature in the story, are given here.

Gladys Currie had told Henry Bennett of the contents of the trunk being burnt 'after being hauled down from its old resting place in the attic'. The attic in whose house – the Langs' in Selkirk, the Curries' at Howford, or Gladys' grandfather Andrew's home in Darnick (he died in 1891) where he had an art studio? It is a matter for speculation. Henry Bennett thought that the burning of the papers as recounted by Miss Currie was one of those simple accidents that do happen now and again and may have accounted for the loss of very valuable material not only to the descendants but also 'the authorities'.

Harry Bennett could not have known, but Kenneth Lupton, in his authoritative work on Mungo Park *The African Traveler* (1979), would note that when a second edition (1815) of Mungo Park's *Travels*, and his *Journal* combined with a *Biographical Memoir* by John Wishaw, was published, Wishaw had collected much other material for Appendices and Addenda. He had obtained this material from the Colonial Office, the Park family, Sir Joseph Banks, Mr Dickson (Mungo Park's brother-in-law) and Sir Walter Scott. Kenneth Lupton's efforts to locate these papers, 'which have never been alluded to since Wishaw used them', was unsuccessful. Wishaw at the time of preparing the 1815 edition of the travels inquired for any remaining fragments relating to the first journey 'but he was rebuffed by Park's brothers'. Had the trunk held the fragments and perhaps the manuscript notes that Wishaw had sought? What a tragic loss to future historians such as Kenneth Lupton.

Henry Bennett tells Miss Currie of another fire in June 1939. 'Ten days ago the Park's old home at Motueka was burned down throwing one of my wife's brothers out (with a big family) just at a time when houses are hard to procure'. This brother of Wikitoria Bennett is Dave, David Raukawa Park, who as a young man lived for a time at Taumata the Love's Petone home, the Dave whose youngest son Tim Park is one reason for my writing of their progenitor Robert Park, and the Dave whose first born Athalie Watt (née Park), to whom this book is jointly dedicated with Bobs Murchison, is the Dave who rescued the kiwi cloak and taiaha and the piano from the conflagration. Had the photo of Robert Park which Ripeka had sent to Motueka been burned in this fire?

In the Motueka fire, continued Henry, 'went another such trunk as we have been discussing, … a box known as 'the camphor trunk' which came to the family from the old country … Well this one [Mungo Park's trunk] at any rate has made its last journey. A little more information and we would have been able to work up a story of the romance of the trunks.'

I think this story of Robert Park, Surveyor, is romance enough. Thank goodness Maori descendants kept alive their particular version of their relationship to Robert Park. Without this there would have been no mystery, and a much less romantic and colourful tale to tell.

The old trunk of Mungo Park was on the move again in 1939 to Taumata, after its long stay in the south. I hope the trunk which is now stored at Te Papa may stand as a symbol for the other traveller, Surveyor Robert Park, and will one day draw the descendants of his three families together in celebration of their common ancestor.

Peter Love - Kaitiaki of Mungo Park's Trunk at the Museum of New Zealand Te Papa Tongarewa, Wellington. October 2008.

Photo Frank Easdale.

WHAKAMAHARATANGA – IN REMEMBRANCE

Of many of those in this story who lie in graveyards and urupa in New Zealand, and in one graveyard in Australia.

In Addington Cemetery, Christchurch

In
Memory
OF
ROBERT PARK
BORN AT GLASGOW OCT 1812
ARRIVED AT WELLINGTON N Z
IN CUBA NOV 1839
DIED AT CHRISTCHURCH MARCH 1870

Sadly Robert Park's tombstone lies fallen on his grave. When restored perhaps the inscription will be corrected. It is not known when the present stone was erected but much later than in the first years following his death. Robert Park's birth date was in January 1812, not October 1812. The arrival of the *Cuba* in Wellington was 4 January 1840, although the ship sighted New Zealand in November 1839.

In Memory
of
CATHERINE EDITH
DEANS
DIED AT RICCARTON
2ND SEPTEMBER 1937
AGED 81 YEARS

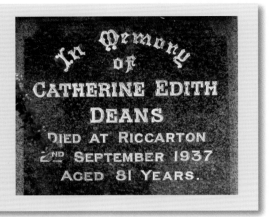

Robert and Marion Park's daughter, Catherine Edith (the third family), together with her husband, John Deans II, and three of their children lie not far away from Edith's father, Robert Park. The inscription for Edith at the back of the column was not able to be photographed so as to show the whole monument.

In the foreground lies Robert Park's tombstone. The column in the distance is the Deans family memorial.

In Bolton Street Cemetery, Wellington

To the left is Mary Anne's tomb-stone with its inscription. To the right is Mary Anne and Robert Park's daughter Mary Jane born 1 January 1842.

IN MEMORY OF
MARY ANNE
Wife of Robt Park Esq
Died in giving birth to a stillborn son
On the 22nd of Jany 1848
Aged 30

Gone is that sunny smile that laughing eye
Mute that sweet voice I lov'd so much to hear
For ever still'd the mother's watchful sigh
For ever dried the wife's consoling tear.

SACRED TO
THE MEMORY OF
MARY
DAUGHTER OF
THE LATE ROBT & MARY ANNE PARK
AND THE BELOVED WIFE OF
J G KINROSS
OF NAPIER
WHO DIED AT WELLINGTON
23rd OCTOBER 1871
MY GRACE IS SUFFICIENT FOR THEE
FOR MY STRENGTH IS MADE PERFECT IN
WEAKNESS.
2 Corinthians 12 v 9.

Did Robert Park engrave this poetic lament to Mary Anne? The style is very like that on his plans and lithographs.

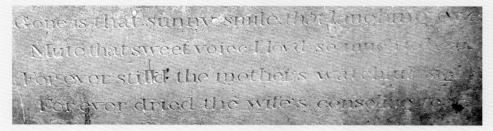

Robert and Mary Anne Park's baby son, Robert Wakefield Park, who died on 1 September 1840, lies in an unmarked grave. Mary Anne Park and her daughter Mary Jane Kinross lie in their original graves, undisturbed by the destructive construction of the motorway. The plots are not far from the boundary of the Park Cottage section.

TO THE MEMORY
OF
MARION
ONLY DAUGHTER OF
ROBERT & MARION HART
OF LONDON
AND WIFE OF THE LATE
ROBERT PARK OF WELLINGTON
AND WINCHMORE CANTERBURY
BORN 24th JUNE 1822
DIED AT WELLINGTON
22nd OCTOBER 1891

Also undisturbed by the motorway, Marion lies in the Hart family plot. A tribute to Marion is in an 1894 eulogy to her brother, Robert Hart, who outlived her by three years. She was 'a peaceful, retiring, God-fearing woman' whose 'devout and assiduous presence' at St Andrew's Church on The Terrace would be remembered by the congregation.

In Otakou Urupa, Otago Harbour

IN MEMORY OF

NGATATA
WHO DIED AT OTAGO
IN THE YEAR 1864
A LEADING CHIEF OF
NGATIAWA
WHO WELCOMED THE PAKEHA
TO COOKS STRAITS
HE WAS THE FATHER OF
THE HON. WI TAKO NGATATA M.L.C.

ERECTED BY THE GOVERNMENT
OF NEW ZEALAND
IN HONOUR OF HIS MEMORY

The original tombstone of Koraraina Taiaroa's father Ngatata i Te Rangi Makore (Ngati Uhiti Hapu) is replaced now with one over his remains bearing the same inscription. The inscription is also in Maori.

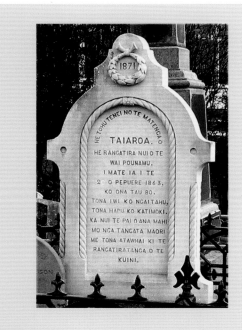

1871	1871
HE TOHU TENEI NO TE MATENGA	A MEMORIAL TO MATENGA
TAIAROA	TAIAROA
HE RANGATIRA NUI O TE	A PARAMOUNT CHIEF OF THE SOUTH
WAI POUNANU	ISLAND
I MATE IA I TE	HE DIED ON THE
2nd O PEPUERE 1863	2ND FEBRUARY 1863
KO ONA TAU 80	AGED 80
TONA IWI KO NGAITAHU	HIS TRIBE IS NGAITAHU
TONA HAPU KO KATIMOKI	HIS HAPU IS KATIMOKI
KA NUI TE PAI O ANA MAHI	HE DID GREAT WORK
MO NGA TANGATA MAORI	FOR THE MAORI PEOPLE
ME TONA ATIWHAI KI TE	AND UPHELD THE
RANGATIRATANGA O TE KUINI	SOVEREIGNTY OF THE QUEEN

Next to him lies a son Hori Kerei Taiaroa, M.H.R.

At Te Puni Street Urupa, Petone

Of those who lie here in Te Puni Street Urupa these people are part of this Park story:

KO TE TOHU TENEI O
HONIANA TE PUNI
RANGATIRA O NGATIAWA
I MATE TE
5 O TIHEMA 1870

TO THE MEMORY OF
HONIANA TE PUNI
A CHIEF OF NGATIAWA
WHO DIED ON 5th DECEMBER 1870

Te Puni's last words were said to have been 'Be kind to my European brothers and sisters, be patient, be tolerant'. Sir Donald McLean and Sir William Fitzherbert were pallbearers at Te Puni's funeral.

The Park Plaques in Te Puni Street Urupa:

IN LOVING MEMORY OF
TERENUI PARK
DAUGHTER OF
TE RANGIAHUTA & TE ANGIOTAU
WIFE OF
ROBERT PARK
MOTHER OF
HUTA PAMARIKI & ANIHAKA

Terenui is said to have died in December 1850. Although her memorial is here her exact burial place in the urupa is unknown.

IN LOVING MEMORY OF
MERENAKO (PARE) PARK
WIFE OF
HUTA PAMARIKI PARK
DIED 27 JUNE 1938 AGED 78 YEARS

IN LOVING MEMORY OF
HENRY (HARRY) PARK
SON OF
HUTA PAMARIKI & MERENAKO PARK
DIED 21 FEBRUARY 1950 AGED 84 YEARS

As Harry was born in 1886 his age was 64 when he died.

IN LOVING MEMORY OF
DAVID RAUKAWA PARK
HUSBAND OF
DULCIE MAY PARK
DIED 5 MAY 1975 AGED 79 YEARS

David was the youngest son of Huta and Pare Park, and father of Athalie, who shares the dedication of this book.

ANI MATENE
TANA WAHINE
I MATE 27 O NGA RA
AKUHATA 1898 ONA TAU 48
NA IHOWA I HOMAI
NA I HOWA I TANGO KIA
WHAKAPAINGA TE INGOA
A IHOWA HOPA 21

ANI MATENE
HIS WIFE
DIED 27th AUGUST 1898 AGED 48
THE LORD GIVETH
AND THE LORD TAKETH AWAY
BLESSED BE THE NAME OF THE LORD. JOB 1
V. 21

HE WHAKAMAHARATANGA
TENEI MO
PAATI MATENE
I MATE 14 O NGA RA
TIHEMA 1897 ONA TAU 42

IN MEMORY OF
PAATI MATENE
DIED 14th OF DECEMBER 1897
AGED 42

Anihaka Matene (née Park) and her husband Paati Matene share this memorial at Te Puni Street Urupa.

Wi Hapi Pakau Love and his wife Ripeka, Rober Park's granddaughter, lie side by side sharing this headstone at Te Puni Street Urupa.

REMEMBRANCE

WI HAPI PAKAU LOVE
BORN DEC. 14th 1878
DIED AUG. 8th 1952

RIPEKA WHARAWHARA LOVE
BORN JUNE 28th 1882
DIED APRIL 6th 1953

E MOE E TE WHARE O TE ATIAWA
PARININIHI KI WAITOTARA KI PITOONE
KO TE PONO, KO TE TIKA , ME TE AROHA
KI TOU HOA TATA, TE MEA NUI O NGA MEA KATOA

SLEEP IN THE HOUSE OF TE ATIAWA
PARININIHI TO WAITOTARA TO PETONE
FOR TRUTH, TO RIGHTEOUSNESS AND THE
MOST IMPORTANT THING OF ALL,
LOVE TOWARDS DEAR FRIENDS

THE STUMP

I was told by a descendant that Paati Matene's father Matene Tauwhare was thought to lie beneath the remains of this tree. Matene Tauwhare's wife Roka (Rose) was a daughter of the ariki, Honiana Te Puni.

HOHEPINE WI TAKO

This red granite memorial stone, simply engraved with only her name, stands out in the Te Puni Street graveyard. Hohepine, the daughter of Wi Tako Ngatata, was married to Taniora (Daniel) Mana Love.

In the Roman Catholic Graveyard, Western Hutt Road, Petone

IN MEMORY OF
WIREMU TAKO NGATATA
OF WELLINGTON
A CHIEF OF NGATIAWA TARANAKI
A MEMBER OF THE LEGISLATIVE COUNCIL OF NEW ZEALAND
HE WAS A LOYAL SUBJRCT OF THE QUEEN, A FIRM FRIEND OF THE EUROPEANS
AND HELD IN HIGH RESPECT BY BOTH RACES
HE DIED IN PITO-ONE ON THE 6th DAY OF NOVEMBER 1887
AGED 87 YEARS.

This celebrated chief at the time of his death had embraced the Roman Catholic religion. The name of Taniora Mana Love 1911, and others, is engraved on the tombstone. Taniora, or Daniel, was the husband of Wi Tako Ngatata's daughter Hohepine, who lies in Te Puni Urupa.

In Motueka Cemetery

IN REMEMBERANCE OF
MERNAKO (PARE) PARK
BELOVED WIFE OF
HUTA PAMARIKI PARK

INTERRED TE PUNI WGTN 1938

IN LOVING MEMORY OF
HUTA PAMARIKI PARK
BELOVED HUSBAND OF
MERENAKO (PARE) PARK
SON OF
ROBERT AND TIRENUI PARK
DIED 17.5.1927

Huta, named for a forebear, Rangiahuta, lies in a family plot in Motueka Public Cemetery. Pare, who died nine years after her husband Huta, is remembered here, though she lies in Te Puni Urupa, Petone. Motueka was Huta and Pare's home for almost 50 years.

In St Faith's Churchyard, Ohinemutu, Rotorua

HEI WHAKAMAHARATANGA
KIA
HANA TE UNUHI MERE PENETI

The weathering of this inscription in Maori makes it difficult to decipher. An inscription in English is at the other end of the tomb.

IN LOVING MEMORY
OF
HANNAH TE UNUHI MARY BENNETT
BELOVED WIFE OF
REVD F. A. BENNETT
ENTERED INTO REST AUGUST 10th 1909
AGED 30 YEARS
*"COME UNTO ME ALL YE THAT LABOUR AND
ARE HEAVY LADEN,
AND I WILL GIVE YOU REST." MATT XI. 28.
"THE MEMORY OF THE JUST IS
BLESSED."PROV.X.7.*

Hana's tomb, built above the restless Ohinemutu earth, is near the entrance to St Faith's Church, which looks over Lake Rotorua. Hana was the eldest daughter of Huta and Pare Park.

In Omaka Cemetery, Blenheim

IN MEMORY OF
ROBERT GEORGE PARK
BORN 19th JULY 1854 DIED 10th MARCH 1905
MARY CAMPBELL PARK
DIED OCT 19th 1896 AGED 31 YEARS
JOHN PARK
BORN 17th SEPT DIED 19th SEPT 1896

Robert George was the son of Robert and Marion Park, and brother of Catherine Edith Deans and Elizabeth Marion Symes. Robert George Park's birth year was 1853. This polished granite headstone appears to have replaced an earlier one.

In Waimari Cemetery, Christchurch

ELIZABETH MARION SYMES
1858 – 1936

Known in the Park family as Minnie, she was the second daughter of Robert and Marion Park, and sister of Robert George Park and Catherine Edith Deans. She was the widow of Dr William Henry Symes of Christchurch.

In Brighton Cemetery, Melbourne, Australia

FRANCIS EDWARD
STEWART
BORN 8th SEPTEMBER 1833
DIED 10th JULY 1904
*BLESSED ARE THE DEAD WHICH DIE IN THE
LORD FOR THEY REST FROM THEIR LABOURS*

ALSO
AGNES
WIFE OF THE ABOVE
BORN 1843 DIED 4th FEB 1927 AGED 84 YEARS

Agnes, the fourth child and third daughter of Robert and Mary Anne Park, had outlived her husband Francis by 23 years. She was much more to her family than this modest footnote may suggest. Agnes was likely to have chosen the quote for her husband's inscription. Indeed, this sentiment could apply so aptly to Agnes as well.

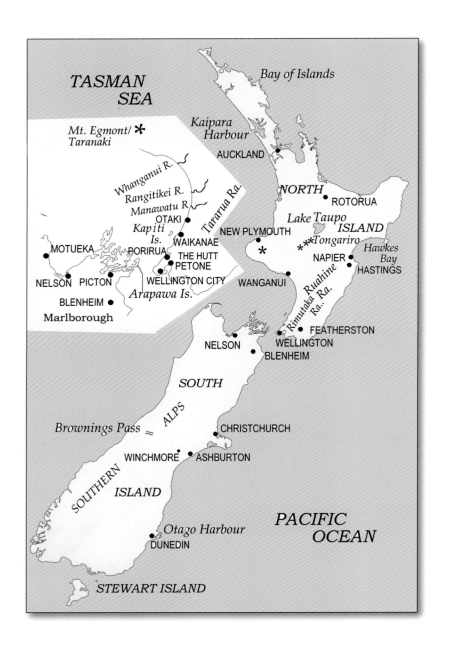

TASMAN
SEA

Bay of Islands

*Kaipara
Harbour*

Mt. Egmont/ ✳
Taranaki

AUCKLAND ●

Whanganui R.
Rangitikei R.
Manawatu R

Tararua Ra.

NORTH ● ROTORUA

Lake Taupo

ISLAND

NEW PLYMOUTH ●

OTAKI
*Kapiti
Is.* WAIKANAE ●
MOTUEKA ● PORIRUA ●
● THE HUTT
● PETONE

✳✳*Tongariro*
✳

NAPIER ●
*Hawkes
Bay*
● HASTINGS

NELSON ● PICTON ●
WELLINGTON CITY
Arapawa Is.

WANGANUI ●

Rimutaka Ra.
Ruahine Ra.

BLENHEIM ●
Marlborough

FEATHERSTON
● WELLINGTON
BLENHEIM

NELSON ●

SOUTH

SOUTHERN

Brownings Pass = ALPS

CHRISTCHURCH ●

WINCHMORE ● ● ASHBURTON

ISLAND

Otago Harbour
DUNEDIN ●

STEWART ISLAND

PACIFIC
OCEAN

TABLE OF DESCENT

The following table is merely a guide to descent from Patrick and Agnes Park of Glasgow covering five generations through their son Matthew to their grandson ROBERT PARK and his progeny in the three families, not all of whom are followed in the story. N.B. Only children who survived infancy figure later in the table.

Further genealogical information may be applied for as follows:

Descendants of Agnes
Stewart Robinson
84 Giacomettis Lane
Coomoora, Victoria, 3461.
Phone 0061 353 482 756
Email: montrose84@bigpond.com

Gillian Webster
1/28 Elm Street Hawthorn
Melbourne 3122 Victoria
Phone 0061 398 535 614
Email: gillwebster@bigpond.com

Descendants of Anihaka
Peter Love
P.O.Box 160
Featherston 5740
New Zealand.
Phone 06 308 6007
Email: love@paradise.net.nz

Descendants of Huta
Mairangi Reiher
168 Commercial Street
Takaka
New Zealand.
Phone 03 525 9793
Email: mairangi.r@xtra.co.nz

Descendants of Marion
Robert George
Heather Murchison
227 Redwood Street
Blenheim 7201
New Zealand.
Phone 03 578 8458
Email: heathermary@gmail.com

Elizabeth Marion
(Manie) Symes:
Michael Symes
18 Ashbourne Street
Burnside
Christchurch
Email: mike@audiovideo.co.nz

Catherine Edith Deans
The Deans family tree
is on page 10 of
'Pioneers of the Plains'
by Gordon Ogilvie.

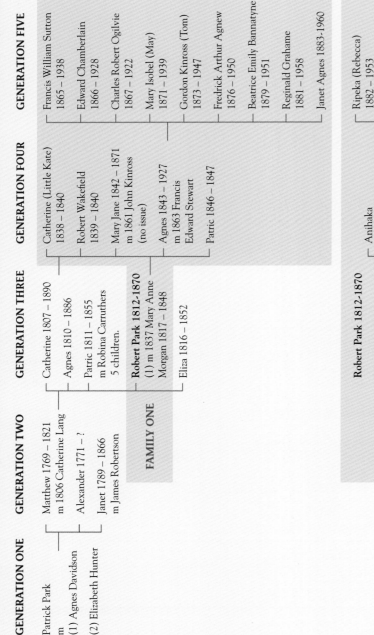

GENERATION ONE

Patrick Park
m
(1) Agnes Davidson
(2) Elizabeth Hunter

GENERATION TWO

Matthew 1769 – 1821
m 1806 Catherine Lang

Alexander 1771 – ?

Janet 1789 – 1866
m James Robertson

GENERATION THREE

Catherine 1807 – 1890

Agnes 1810 – 1886

Patric 1811 – 1855
m Robina Carruthers
5 children.

Robert Park 1812-1870
(1) m 1837 Mary Anne
Morgan 1817 – 1848

Eliza 1816 – 1852

FAMILY ONE

GENERATION FOUR

Catherine (Little Kate)
1838 – 1840

Robert Wakefield
1839 – 1840

Mary Jane 1842 – 1871
m 1861 John Kinross
(no issue)

Agnes 1843 – 1927
m 1863 Francis
Edward Stewart

Patric 1846 – 1847

GENERATION FIVE

Francis William Sutton
1865 – 1938

Edward Chamberlain
1866 – 1928

Charles Robert Ogilvie
1867 – 1922

Mary Isobel (May)
1871 – 1939

Gordon Kinross (Tom)
1873 – 1947

Fredrick Arthur Agnew
1876 – 1950

Beatrice Emily Bannatyne
1879 – 1951

Reginald Grahame
1881 – 1958

Janet Agnes 1883-1960

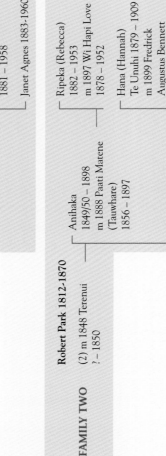

Robert Park 1812-1870
(2) m 1848 Terenui
? – 1850

FAMILY TWO

Anihaka
1849/50 – 1898
m 1888 Paati Matene
(Tauwhare)
1856 – 1897

Huta Pamariki
1850 – 1927
m. 1877 Merenako
(Pare) Kitakita
1860 – 1938

Ripeka (Rebecca)
1882 – 1953
m 1897 Wi Hapi Love
1878 – 1952

Hana (Hannah)
Te Unuhi 1879 – 1909
m 1899 Fredrick
Augustus Bennett
1872 – 1950

Henry (Harry) Selwyn
1886 – 1950
m Ewa Wirepa

Wikitoria (Victoria)
Te Amohau 1888 – 1975
m Henry Dargaville
Bennett

Rawiri (Dave) Raukawa
m Dulcie Fisher
*(Their daughter was Athalie
Eleanor Te Uria Watt 1925 –
2007. See Dedication.)*

FAMILY THREE

Robert Park 1812 – 1870
m 1852 Marion Hart
1823 – 1891

Robert George
1853 – 1905
m 1886 Mary Campbell
Ferguson
1865 – 1896

- Robert 1886 – 1917
- Mary (Molly) Roberta
  1889 – 1968
  m 1913 Ken Murchison
  1887 – 1949
  (Their son was Robert (Bobs)
  John Sinclair 1916 – 2007.
  See Dedication.)
- George Reginald
  1893 – 1944

Catherine Edith
1856 – 1937
m 1879 John Deans (II)
1853 – 1902

- John (III) 1880 – 1974
- Marion 1881 – 1970
- Robert George
  1884 – 1908
- James 1885 – 1963
- Catherine 1886 – 1901
- William 1888 – 1890
- Alexander 1890 – 1917
- Douglas 1892 – 1982
- Colin 1894 – 1973
- Violet 1896 – 1901
- Stuart Maxwell
  1897 – 1986

Elizabeth Marion
(Minnie)1858 – 1936
m 1878 William Henry
Symes 1843 – 1905

- Langford Park
  1879 – 1965
- Robert Cracroft McLean
  1881 –
- Marion Dorothea
  1884 – 1978

GLOSSARY

Ariki	Paramount chief
Freits	Omens (Gaelic)
Hikoi	Trek
Kaitiaki	Guardian
Kainga	Unfortified village
Kuia	Old woman
Pā	Fortified village
Plenishings	The full furnishings of a house, full household effects
Piupiu	Flax skirt
Taua	War party
Taonga	Treasures
Utu	Satisfaction, price, reward, return
Whakapapa	Genealogy, family tree
Wharenui	Meeting house

ABBREVIATIONS

A.T.L.	Alexander Turnbull Library. National Library of New Zealand Te Puna Matauranga o Aotearoa
DOC	Department of Conservation
LINZ	Land Information New Zealand
MHR	Member of House of Representatives
MLC	Member of Legislative Council
N.Z.I.S.	New Zealand Institute of Surveyors
U.P.	University Press, e.g. Oxford University Press

BIBLIOGRAPHY

PUBLICATIONS

Books

Acland L.G.D.	*The Early Canterbury Runs*. 1930 4th edn. Whitcoulls Ltd. 1975.
Alington M.A.	*Unquiet Earth*. Wellington City Council 1978.
Ault H.F.	*The Nelson Narrative*. Anglican Diocese of Nelson 1958.
Caughey Angela	*The Interpreter*. David Bateman 1998.
Cavanagh T.	*Public Sculpture of Liverpool*. Liverpool U.P. 1997.
Chapple L.J.B.and H.C.Veitch	*Wanganui*. Hawera Star Publishing Co. 1939.
Church Ian N.	*Port Chalmers and its People*. Otago Heritage Books 1994.
Clarke Sandra	*Nga Tupuna o Te Whanganui-a-Tara*. Wellington City Council and Wellington Tenths Trust 1995.
Cowan James	*Sir Donald McLean*. A.H. & A.W. Reed 1940.
Crawford J.C.	*Recollections of Travel in New Zealand and Australia*. London 1880.
Deans John	*Pioneers of Canterbury*. A.H. & A.W. Reed 1937.
Deans Jane	*Letters to My Grandchildren*. Kiwi Publishers 3rd edn Christchurch 1995.
Dieffenbach Ernst	*Travels in New Zealand* Vol. 1. London 1843 Capper Press reprint 1974.
Downes T.W.	*Old Whanganui*. W. Parkinson Hawera 1915.
Easdale Nola	*Kairuri The Measurer of Land*. Highgate/Price Millburn Petone 1988.
EvisonHarry C.	*The Ngai Tahu Deeds*. Canterbury U.P. 2000.
Fargher Ray	*The Best Man Who Ever Served the Crown*. Victoria U.P. 2007.
Gibbon Lewis Grassic	*Niger: The Life of Mungo Park*. Edinburgh 1934.
Godley Charlotte	*Letters from Early New Zealand*. Whitcombe & Tombs Christchurch 1951.
Greenaway Richard	'Rich man, poor man...' in a *Biography of Canterbury Personalities*. Christchurch City Council 2000.
Grover Ray	*Cork of War*. John McIndoe Dunedin 1982.
Heaphy Charles	*A Residence in New Zealand*. London 1842 Hocken Library Facsimile No. 7 1968.
Hewson A.	*Early Days in Ashburton County*. Ashburton Mail 1918 Republished 1996 Ashburton Museum and Historical Society Inc.
Hocken T.M.	*The Early History of New Zealand*. Government Printer 1914.
Hutt News Print	*Petone West School Golden Jubilee 1909-1959*.
Irvine-Smith F.L.	*The Streets of My City*. A.H. & A.W. Reed Wellington [1948].
Johnston Sir Harry	*Pioneers in West Africa*. London 1912.
Jordan F.S.	*Early Days in Motueka*. n.d. Copy from Nelson Provincial Museum.
Keene Howard	*Going for Gold*. Department of Conservation Canterbury Conservancy 1972.

Kerr Donald Jackson	*Amassing Treasure for all Times. Sir George Grey. Colonial Bookman and Collector* Otago U.P. 2006
Keyse Captain G.J.	*Pilots Otago Harbour/The Port of Otago A Nautical Diary.* Typescript 1989.
Lake Coleridge Tourism Group	*West of Windwhistle.* 2005.
Lawn C.A.	*Pioneer Land Surveyors of New Zealand.* N.Z.I.S. 1977
Lockhart J.G.	*Life of Sir Walter Scott..* Edinburgh 1837-38.
Lupton Kenneth	*Mungo Park, The African Traveler.* Oxford U.P. 1979.
May Philip R.	*The West Coast Gold Rushes.* Pegasus Press Christchurch 1962.
McGregor Miriam	*Early Stations of Hawke's Bay.* A.H. & A.W. Reed 1970.
McLintock A.H.	*The Port of Otago.* Whitcombe & Tombs Ltd. 1951.
McMorran Barbara	*Octavius Hadfield.* Author Wellington 1969.
Macmorran George	*Some Schools and Schoolmasters of Early Wellington.* S. & G.W. Mackey 1900.
Main William	*Wellington Through a Victorian Lens.* Millwood Press Wellington 1972.
Milner J. and Brierley O.W.	*The Cruise of the Galatea.* London 1869.
Mitchell Hilary & John	*Te Ara Hou* Vols I & II. Huia Publishers Wellington 2004, 2007.
Money Charles	*Knocking About in New Zealand* 1871 Capper Press reprint 1972.
Mooney K and Henderson M.	*A Picture Book of Old Hawkes Bay.* Benton Ross Ltd. Auckland 1984.
Morley W.	*The History of Methodism in New Zealand.* 1900.
McLintock A.H.	*The Port of Otago.* Whitcombe & Tombs 1951.
Nicholson W.B. ed.	*Petone's First Hundred Years … 1840-1940.* Petone Borough Council 1940.
Ogilvie Gordon	*Pioneers of the Plains The Deans of Canterbury.* Shoal Bay Press 1996.
Park Mungo	*Travels in the Interior Districts of Africa, … 1795,1796 and 1797.* London 1799.
Pascoe John	*Unclimbed New Zealand.* Allen & Unwin London 1939.
Patterson B.R.	'A Queer Cantankerous Lot' in *Making of Wellington.* Ed. D.A. Hamer and R.Nicholls Victoria U.P 1990.
Read Benedict	*Victorian Sculpture.* Yale U.P. 1982.
Rochfort John	*Adventures of a Surveyor in New Zealand.* [London 1853?] Capper Press reprint 1974.
Scotter W.H.	*Ashburton.* Ashburton Borough and County Councils 1972.
Stewart Jean	*Scribblers.* Kingswood Press Queensland Australia 2007.
Taylor Nancy M. ed.	*The Journal of Ensign Best.* Government Printer 1966.
Taylor W.A.	*Lore and History of the South Island Maori.* [1950] Facsimile edition 2001 Kiwi Publishers Christchurch.
Temple Philip	*A Sort of Conscience: The Wakefields.* Auckland U.P. 2002.
Wakefield E.J.	*Adventure in New Zealand* Vols 1 & 2 London 1845. Facsimile Wilson & Horton Ltd. *Illustrations to Adventure in New Zealand.* Smith, Elder London 1845.
Ward Louis E.	*Early Wellington.* Whitcombe & Tombs 1928. Capper Press reprint 1975.
Wards Ian	*The Shadow of the Land.* Government Printer 1968.
Warren Joan & Parata, Muri.	*Te Tatau o te Po History 75th Jubilee.* A. Fraser 2008.
Wilson J.G.	*The Founding of Hawke's Bay.* Daily Telegraph Co. Ltd Napier 1951. *A History of Hawke's Bay.* 1939 Capper Press reprint 1976.
Worsdall Frank	*The Glasgow Tenement.* Richard Drew Glasgow 1989.

Periodicals

The Builder Vol IX January 1851 (U K).
The Borders Magazine Vols XI 1906 and XXV 1920. Edinburgh.

Proceedings of the Berwickshire Naturalists' Club 1882-1884. Alnwick 1885. (From Scottish Borders Library Selkirk).
Canterbury Mountaineer No. 18 1948-49.
New Zealand Alpine Journal Vols 18 and 19 1933-1938
Church Messenger Nelson Diocese 1871-1890 Synod Report 1881.
New Zealand Geological Survey Bulletin No. 1 (New Series). Department of Mines Government Printer 1906.
The Perfect Touch. Exhibition Publication. Mornington Peninsula Regional Gallery Melbourne 2003.

Newspapers

Papers Past (Online) National Library of New Zealand.
New Zealand Gazette & Wellington Spectator 1840-1844.
New Zealand Spectator & Cook's Strait Guardian 1844-1854.
Wellington Evening Post March 1870, February 1950, August 1952, November 1973.
New Zealand Free Lance January 1939.
Lyttelton Times February 1864, July 1865, March 1870, February 1877, February 1886, September 1888, July 1907, March 1927.
Motueka Star May 1927.
Nelson Evening Mail September 1877.
Ashburton Guardian December 1989.

Official Sources

Taranaki Provincial Gazette 1874/75.
Appendices to Journals of the House of Representatives 1852.
Electoral Rolls.
British and Scottish Census (Online) 1841-1881.
Gazettes 1841, 1842. Government Press Auckland 1843.
Proceedings – Provincial Council of Canterbury 1865.
Acts and Proceedings Wellington Provincial Council 1854-1856.
New Zealand Gazettes 1854-1859.

Dictionaries, Encyclopedia, Directories

Dictionary of National Biography London 1895.
Oxford Dictionary of National Biography Oxford U.P. 2004-8
Australian Dictionary of Biography (Online edition).
Dictionary of New Zealand Biography 1940.
Southern People. A Dictionary of Otago and Southland Biography 1998.
Dictionary of New Zealand Biography 1990-2000.
Te Ao Hou National Library (Online).
Encylopaedia of New Zealand 1966.
G. R. Macdonald Dictionary of Canterbury Biographies Canterbury Museum.
Dictionary of Scottish Art and Architecture 1988.
Wises Directories 1860-1942.
Dictionary of New Zealand Biography (Online) Ministry for Culture and Heritage.
Wikipedia (Online).

GENERAL MANUSCRIPT SOURCES

Canterbury Museum

Deans Family Papers.

Archives New Zealand / Te Rua Mahara o te Kawanatanga

Canterbury Branch
CH 171 A713/1870
CH 214 Box 108/829
CH 290 18/38 fol. 6, 42/20 fol. 218
Wellington Office
Land Information New Zealand, National Office, Series 8012, Acc. W5279

National Library of Scotland

Acc. No 10098 Vols 1 & 2
On deposit from Inverness Courier
Letter Robert Park to Patric Park

Hocken Library

F & J 2/12
Biographical notes on Robert Park. Probably written by son Robert George Park prior to 1905.
Entered by Dr. Hocken. Park's date of birth incorrect (entered in another hand).
Misc MS-184
'Mungo Park History'. Notes by Harry Park 1939.
Letters from Ripeka Love and H.D. Bennett to Miss Gladys Currie 1939, 1940. Corr. Thompson with
Hocken Librarian 1973 (Date of deposit of above papers).
MS- 0439/014 Baptisms, Deaths, Marriages Register to 1848.
MS- 0534/023, 025 Watkins. Watkins Burial Register and BDM 1840-1863.
MS- 0440/017 Creed, Charles Letters.
Misc MS- 0502 Early Maori Lay Ministers.

Auckland City Libraries

GL- G37 (5)
GL- G37 (8)
GL- NZ N8 (2)
GL- W2- E7 (37)
GL- NZ T5A (8)
Grey Letters. Special Collections.

Alexander Turnbull Library

McLean Family Papers (MS Group 1556)
MS-Papers-0032 - 0491 Robert Park to Donald McLean
                           0811 Catherine McLean (later Hart) to Donald McLean
                           0812 Robert Hart Correspondence

0813 Robert Hart Correspondence
0961 Marion Park to Annabella McLean
0826-0828 Susan Strang (later McLean) to Donald McLean (Transcribed by Marsha Macdonald)
0998 Marion Park to Susan McLean
New Zealand Journal Micro MS 0518 Vols 1-12 1840-1852
Petre, Mary Eleanor Journal MS 2001-060-08
Letters – Kate Hadfield. Reminiscences of Bishop Hadfield Otaki School Affairs, Correspondence, Accounts MS
    Papers 0139 fol. 11-27
Letters – Mary Williams Otaki MS Papers 0213 – 04.
Baptisms 1839–1844, Marriages 1841-1864 Micro MS 0230-1
Wellington Maori Pastorate Registers. Micro MS-0883
Register BMB Micro MS-0252-1A
Mantell Family Papers. MS Papers 0083 Dillon Bell to Mantell.
Wakefield, E.J. Diary MS-2208
MS- Papers-1534 Diary William Mein Smith
MS- Papers-4212 Newberry A.R. Diary [Brownings Pass] 1865
New Zealand Company Principal Surveyor Letterbook 1839-1843
William Mein Smith and Samuel Brees Micro-MS-0264

Anglican Centre Nelson

Baptism, Marriage & Burial Registers

Land Information New Zealand

Christchurch   F.Bs. 177 O.S., 178 O.S. Robert Park; 5 O.S. Robert Browning
Wellington   F.B. 43, F.B. 44 Robert Park
Dunedin   F.B. 149A Greenlaw W.

Riccarton Bush Trust

Deans Family Papers Boxes 1, 2, 3 (Disc 004), 6 and uncatalogued notes

OTHER SOURCES

BBC History Homepages (Online).
Cemetery Records All Souls Kensal Green London.
British and Scottish Census 1841-1881 (Online).
Baptism, Marriage, Burial Registers Methodist Church of New Zealand, Christchurch.
Baptism, Marriage, Burial Registers Anglican Centre, Nelson.
Christchurch City Council Cemeteries Database (Online)
Family Records (Latterday Saints) (Online)
Waitangi Tribunal Briefs of Evidence 2003 of Athalie Eleanor te Uira Park and Mairangi Reiher.
Personal Communications with Family Members – See Acknowledgements.

ACKNOWLEDGEMENTS

So much help has been given by so many. One of the greatest pleasures of the research has been the contact with descendants of Robert Park's three families.

They have all been unfailingly helpful, interested in the project, and generous in sharing their knowledge of family lore and their own research. Early on, Tim Park (second family) sent much material, gathered largely from his older sister Athalie. The enthusiasm and knowledge of this lady (now sadly deceased) and the continuing support of her partner Jack was a contribution fundamental and essential. As was that of Heather Murchison (third family), daughter of the late Bobs Murchison, an inveterate collector of family memorabilia. A treasure trove from both sources came to me with an abundance of photos and screeds of notes. And then from the first family in Australia came more photos, more tales, and the file of their letters and emails grew. Phone calls brought their warm interest closer, when I spoke with Gillian Webster, Stewart Robinson and Dr June Cumbrae-Stewart of Tasmania. Barry Cairns was also a useful contact.

The Scottish Connection – so very confused, but with the professional help of Dr Betty Iggo of Edinburgh, the Robert Park inheritance originating in Glasgow began to emerge. I am grateful to an old friend Ailsa Matheson for alerting me to Betty and her talent. Heather Murchison during a visit to Scotland last year was able to further clarify some aspects and take some photos in the Selkirk area and Edinburgh. Her vital interest and support has never flagged and a friendship I value has developed.

Monsignor Bennett (second family, a Bennett historian) along with Jack Webber advised me to be in touch with Nelson descendants. A most rewarding visit resulted. Further photos and stories from, and friends in, Mairangi Reiher, Ramari and the Rev. Andy Joseph, and Judi Billens. Thanks to Ashley Spice of the Mokena family, which is connected to Ahurewa Church, Motueka, who did translations for Whakamaharatanga. There were pleasant and helpful conversations with others in the North Island, Pam Evans (Athalie and Tim Park's sister), Nui and Ralph Biss, the late Muri Parata, Joan Warren and Julie Temple. James Wheeler took me to a Tenths meeting where I was introduced to Peter Love. Peter has, with great generosity, sent me treasured original photos to copy which had once hung in Taumata . (Incidentally Love children were schoolmates of my mother at Petone West School, below Taumata, and also later of my cousin June, and I may claim in my youth to have danced with one of the Love boys!) With Peter, too, I had the thrill of viewing Mungo Park's trunk at Te Papa.

The third family. Heather Murchison I have thanked already, but I must add thanks to her aunt Catherine McQueen for information on Glenthorne, and to her son Donald McQueen who pointed to Robert Park's true birth date. Then there is that prolific family, the Deans of Canterbury. I have had a happy association with sculptor Paul Deans and his venerable artist father Austen Deans who were the source of an exciting find of further Park paintings. They have been greatly interested and supportive. Charles Deans was instrumental in my gaining access to the archive at Riccarton House where there were further discoveries of drawings, paintings and photos made with the helpful co-operation of the Manager, Rob Dally. At lunch at Riccarton House, too, we talked with Robin Park, visiting from Thames, and his wife Helen. They are the keepers of the Park family seal and are well versed in family genealogy. Mike Symes helped to fill in some gaps in his branch. And June Deans who has three pastels by that genius granddaughter of Robert Park's first family, kindly allowed my husband to photograph them. As did Judy Deans with the Robert Park sketches in the keeping of her father Patric Deans.

The institutions visited or consulted were many, in Scotland and in New Zealand. I must thank the staff of the Heritage Hub in Hawick, Scotland, and in particular Helen

Darling of the Scottish Borders Council Library in Selkirk who sent so promptly and happily all that I asked for concerning the Currie family. I am grateful to Nigel Sharp, Parks Development Officer with the Liverpool City Council, who found the whereabouts of the Patric Park sculpture of 'Little Kate' and took and sent photographs. From the Mitchell Library, Glasgow, Enda Ryan supplied some genealogical notes. Ulrike Hogg, and Sheila Robinson of the National Library of Scotland were instrumental in enabling the pastel self-portrait of sculptor Patric Park to be reproduced. Thank you both.

To begin in the north with the New Zealand institutions. Kate de Courcy, Manuscripts Librarian at Auckland Public Libraries could not have been more helpful with the Park sketches in the Grey Collection. Thanks to her and her colleagues Keith Giles and Annette Hay (digital photography) there are now excellent reproductions in the book of many of the sketches in his sketch book. At Auckland Museum Library Gordon Maitland, expert on old photos, was able to identify one such as an ambrotype. Judith Bright, Kinder Library, St John's Theological College, sent information on Bishop Hadfield and Tamihana Rauparaha.

In Wellington, there was the National Library, especially the Alexander Turnbull Library. As usual, staff in Manuscripts have assisted in looking up the sometimes complex referencing. In Photographs, albums were explored and photos reproduced with the help of Kirsty Willis. Dave Small, Curator of the Cartographic Collection, willingly helped in finding the maps and plans needed. To Marian Minson, Curator of Drawings and Prints, who was, as in the past, of outstanding assistance, my grateful thanks – as always. Through Marsha Donaldson, who had transcribed the Susan Strang/McLean letters in the McLean Papers for Turnbull, another window was opened on the personalities of Robert Park and Marion Hart (third family) to add to my former search of the McLean Papers. Thank you Marsha for this unsuspected treasure. Peter Corbett at Land Information New Zealand helped to access Park Field Books, and Wendy Shaw, Secretary of the New Zealand Geographic Board, tracked down some plans and helped solve a dilemma over names. Carolyn McGill, Collections Manager of History at Te Papa, unveiled Mungo Park's trunk, and my husband photographed it. Staff at National Archives found and allowed photos of the Mohaka deeds and maps and a Wanganui map.

Nelson Provincial Museum yielded photos, some printed material, and a plan. My thanks to the Collections Manager of Photographs, Anne McEwan, and to Anna Wilkinson, Librarian/Archivist, for their patient help. At the Nelson Anglican Centre Anita Jones is another to thank for her willing and kindly assistance.

In Christchurch, at Central Library, Christchurch City Libraries, Richard Greenaway, Gillian Roncelli and Gail Ross all helped in various ways. Ross Moulton, former Chief Surveyor, at Land Information New Zealand, led a way through the particularities of the Christchurch land records. A thank you to the staff at National Archives, Christchurch, in particular the Regional Archivist, Chris Adam. Ian Hill of the Historic Heritage section of the Department of Conservation was of great practical assistance – thank you. At Canterbury Museum there was the kind help of Jane McKnight, Curator of Pictorial Collections, and Michelle Lambert, with excellent images of Park paintings from Katie Wilson, Image Technician. Katie also photographed Edith Deans' wedding dress which had been arranged by Jennifer Quérée and Natalie Cadenhead of Decorative Arts. Jo Smith, Archivist for the Methodist Church of New Zealand, helped with registers to determine facts of the Park's Dunedin sojourn.

Michael Hanrahan, Curator of Ashburton Museum, shared his knowledge of the town and Winchmore station, and provided a copy of part of the Park map. In Dunedin, Field Books were photographed at Land Information New Zealand. And lastly thanks to staff at Hocken Library for information, and to Sharon Dell, Hocken Librarian, for scotching those nasty rumours about Mr Park.

Others who have been of much assistance were Robin Watt, Cultural Heritage and Museum Consultants, who set me on the right course initially to the whereabouts of Mungo Park's trunk. Thanks to Angela Caughey an old friend from whom I had useful information sourced for her book *The Interpreter*. Marg and Bob Verrall, the welcoming owners of the present Winchmore property, produced a Park watercolour of the old house, and showed photos copied from those with Grant Hart of

Christchurch. Through Dr Jane Batchelor, a descendant of Captain William Thomson, Huta Park's time as a pilot at Otago Heads was confirmed.

A thank you also to archaeologist daughter Sheridan Easdale in Dunedin who was often of help in searching some tricky aspects of the story at Hocken Library. What would I have done without my husband Frank, who patiently pursued, at my behest, genealogical details on the internet, and put on disc the dozens of photos and paintings of which he had made digital images. He sketched the maps, an essential aid for the reader. And he spent hours typing up the drafts of the chapters from my handwritten script, letting me get on with writing the next chapter. A great time saver, when all I had to do then was correct and edit, instead of doing my one or sometimes two finger effort. He was with me, too, when we met family members. This, though, I believe he enjoyed as much as I did. What was best perhaps was being able to discuss with him the puzzles, which were many, as he came to know the cast; a great help in reaching conclusions, especially those of geographical aspect.

The idea of album pages to accommodate the numerous sketches and photographs was a happy inspiration of Book Design Limited.

And lastly to historian, Dr John Wilson, friend and thoughtful editor, who didn't hesitate in saying 'Yes' when asked whether this book might be published under his imprint of Te Waihora Press, a big Thank You.

INDEX OF PEOPLE

**This Index lists personal names in chapters 1 to 16.
The numbers in italics relate to illustrations.**

276